PARANORMAL NIAGARA

CASES OF THE MYSTERIOUS AND MACABRE

PETER ANDREW SACCO

Copyright © 2013 Peter Andrew Sacco

ISBN 978-1-62646-702-6

All rights reserved. No part of this publication may be reproduced, stored in a retrieval system, or transmitted in any form or by any means, electronic, mechanical, recording or otherwise, without the prior written permission of the author.

Published by BookLocker.com, Inc., Bradenton, Florida.

Printed in the United States of America.

BookLocker.com, Inc.
2013

First Edition

ACKNOWLEDGEMENTS

This book would not be possible with all the help I have had from the following folks:

Thank you to Erica Benedikty and the team at TV Cogeco for the amazing second season of taping Niagara's Most Haunted. A sincere thanks to Robert "Scotty" Crawford for his interview, information and copies of reports from the 1970 'Poltergeist' case in St. Catharines. Thank you to Mayor Vance Badawey of Port Colborne for his help at various locations and setting up interviews. Thank you to Eva Nicklas and the information she provided me with for Lewiston, NY locations. A special thanks to David "Buck" Rodgers for the exceptional help with all the shoots and information gathering sessions!

DISCLAIMER

The following information in this book was gathered and collected through interviews with willing participants, newspaper clippings and media interviews. Several names have been changed or not used to protect individual identities and locations. The information in this book was collected from reputable individuals and I am not one to judge, accept or refute what they have told me. Final conclusions are left to the reader.

I have also chosen not to disclose the actual location of the "Possession Case" mentioned in this book, even though it is and has been made known in the media. I have not and will not describe or offer the location of the "Haunted House" in this book to anyone, outside of those who provided me with interviews or helped find information to maintain the privacy of the individuals who now own the house. Also, I will never mention the names of those involved in the "Phantom Case", as that was discussed when these folks agreed to be interviewed. I respect their privacy and their wishes. Thank you.

CHAPTERS

INTRODUCTION.. 1
CHAPTER ONE - POLTERGEIST OR POSSESSION?...................... 3
CHAPTER TWO - AN EVIL HAUNTED HOUSE............................ 19
CHAPTER THREE - HAUNTED TREES AND FORESTS 29
CHAPTER FOUR - ORBS AT DECEW FALLS 39
CHAPTER FIVE - DO PHANTOMS REALLY EXIST?................... 51
CHAPTER SIX - A HAUNTED THEATRE 63
CHAPTER SEVEN - AN OLD AND HAUNTED OPERA HALL..... 71
CHAPTER EIGHT - WHAT THE EXPERTS SAY, YOU DECIDE!. 81
EXCERPT FROM FEAR FACTORS: THE CLOSET......................... 93

INTRODUCTION

I am the host of the local TV series *Niagara's Most Haunted*, now in its second season. I created the series based on my factual book of the same name *Niagara's Most Haunted: Legends and Myths*. I live in one of the most beautiful places in the entire world--The Niagara Region. Sure it boasts being the home to one of the most amazing wonders of the world. It has some of the most eye-popping scenery, both naturally created and man-made as well. It is also the home of the most historical, bloody battles in North America history, the War of 1812. Some experts in the field of paranormal research, ghost investigation, and pseudo-psychological research claim that the Niagara Region is a hot bed for paranormal and haunted activities. Furthermore, some claim that Niagara on the Lake is the most haunted town in North America! Is it any wonder people come to try and see ghosts on the many "ghost walks" made available for the curious?

I have been asked many times as to whether or not I believe or disbelieve. Often times I sit on the fence and answer, "I don't know!" I know, I am a coward perhaps more so when it comes to me answering questions about my beliefs on ghosts versus actually going to these "haunted" places, which I might add is very fun! I must admit, being a "man of science" and "needing to see it to believe it" when it comes to this stuff, I have actually learned a lot about things that supposedly go "bump in the night" through filming this series.

My production team and I have gone through many "haunted" places and have been fortunate to interview some really cool, interesting, and informed people. After all, when you have so many historical sites linked to the War of 1812, there is a lot of "history" linked to these sites and of course...ghost stories! If you read my *book Niagara's Most Haunted: Legends and Myths*, you will be informed, entertained, and enlightened...very enlightened!

This is a different book you are about to read as it focuses on several unique, bizarre stories/cases that have haunted the Niagara Region for many decades. These stories are not the popular War of 1812 haunted location variety, rather they are the ones "shrouded" in secrecy, or have details missing, inconclusive outcomes, or no one is talking. I hope you will enjoy reading this fun little book as it was very fun writing it!

CHAPTER ONE

POLTERGEIST OR POSSESSION?

CASES OF THE MYSTERIOUS AND MACABRE

Being the host of the TV series *Niagara's Most Haunted* has given me the opportunity to hear about many things, some stranger than others. Then there are some things that are just plain scary when you hear about them. The famous case which haunted the Niagara Region, namely St. Catharines, Ontario back in 1970, still haunts us today, some people more than others. The unusual thing about this case was that it didn't involve ghosts or apparitions, rather poltergeists...and some believe demons!

I sat down with retired police officer Bob "Scotty" Crawford after having him on my TV show to discuss the famous case from 1970. As Bob put it, "Everyone started calling me Scotty, because of my accent, and the name stuck!" Bob is Scottish, and I can only imagine his accent was a little thicker back in 1970, not too long removed from Scotland, and also due to what he was witnessing in St. Catharines.

Years ago I got to know another retired police officer involved in that case, who did a TV interview with a friend of mine from that same case. I had heard of the case and only had sketchy details. When this fellow started discussing what happened with the case, I was intrigued, shocked, and even a part of me wallowed in disbelief. Little did I know that more than 10 years later I would be sitting down with Bob, and he would be telling me more, a whole lot more which would not only corroborate what this other cop had told me, but remove any scepticism I might have possessed.

Forty-three years later, Bob is older now. Some of his experiences from that incident were a little vague. Perhaps it was due to the detailed questions I was asking. After all I was really going after detailed answers. Bob did not disappoint. Being a man of science (social psychologist), I wanted just the facts "Jack"! That is what I am about to give you -- the facts that Bob gave me, the facts I got from other cops associated with the case, the facts from police reports that Bob gave me, and some facts on what experts believe about similar situations such as the one that occurred in St. Catharines, Ontario.

I am going to discuss Bob's story one-on-one now, with just "the facts.". I will also add to Bob's story the information I received years back from another cop on the case. Later in the book, I will define and discuss the parameters of poltergeists, demonic possessions, as well as paranormal research and let you decide what you really think happened there.

On the set with retired police officer Robert "Scotty" Crawford discussing the 1970 case for an episode of Niagara's Most Haunted.

The insanity (anomaly) according to Bob started in February 1970. He recalled it to be around the 6th day of the month. That put this event almost in the middle of winter, cold, dark and bleak which some believe the month of February to be. With the timing of the event, that would mean most people would have their windows closed and heaters running. Back in the day, many heating systems in apartment buildings where this took place had hot water heating units. The reason I add this is because Bob and I discussed the possibility of random "noises", such as the rattling and clicking of pipes contributing to the "banging" noises. You see, this event originally began as noises....very loud and annoying noises which disrupted other people in the building and why Bob thought he was responding to a domestic dispute or familial squabble when he first received the call to go to the apartment in St. Catharines.

Interestingly, by its mainstream definition, "poltergeist" means "noisy spirit". Eventually, Bob and the folks involved in the case would attribute the noise and chaos to a poltergeist--after all it was sure as hell making a lot of noise! We will get to that later, but for now, Bob discussed the first visit to the apartment.

"Friends of the family first called the police," he told me. Apparently there would be loud knocking coming through the walls. When I asked him if he thought that family members in other rooms or neighbours in other apartments were making a ruckus, he flatly said, "No!" The noises seemed to be "in the walls" and were being generated that way. Could it have been mice, rats, squirrels, or raccoons seeking refuge in the walls for the winter to avoid the cold? He told me that the sounds were too distinct and methodical to be rodents causing the problem. I further asked him to discuss the knocks and he told me they were very loud and rhythmic. This made me wonder, so I asked the question, "Did the knocks continually come in threes?" Bob thought for a moment before nodding and responding, "Yes, I never really thought about it that way before, but now that you mention it, the knocks were coming in rhythmic threes!" I was curious about this as I had read something a while back from someone who investigated many of these instances, and he cited "3's" was a popular rhythm. I will discuss this later on.

Being the first responding officer, Bob sat with the family for a bit after he was invited in to get their collective stories as to why the noises were occurring. Bob stated he was there to warn them to stop making the disruptive noises as it was disturbing the other neighbours, but his attitude and opinion of the situation would change rather quickly.

"First off, the mother was very worried about what was happening. She was worried that whatever was happening, or whatever 'thing' it was, was attacking her son," recalled Bob. "On the other hand, her husband, who was also the boy's father, was pretty laid back and trying to make sense of what was really happening."

Bob stated that he kept an open mind as he was listening to their stories. *In the back of one's mind you kind of need to see it to believe it*, he thought to himself. That's when he would get a taste of his own experience with the paranormal!

Bob was from Scotland. He reminded me that Scotland is much older than Canada, and there is much more folklore, legends, and ghost stories that "haunt" Scotland. He was sure to include the Loch Ness monster Nessie! With that said, he believed that "this kind of stuff" is possible and exists if legends endure that long. Furthermore, he believed if he did see it, it wouldn't really phase him after all he heard about this kind of stuff his whole young life to that point. So when the chair with the boy sitting in it picked up and suddenly moved the boy across the room when Bob was speaking with the parents, he was only mildly "shocked." Bob stated that this would be only the first of the random events involving the boy, ones that would usually have the kid getting pushed or literally "bullied" by some unknown entity.

The chair incidents were not only common to Bob, but to other police officers as well who had shown up to the apartment. A police officer, Mike, went through his experience in vivid detail. The detail was so amazing that Maple Tree Productions, a Canadian production company producing documentaries, did a re-enactment involving the boy and the chair.

As Mike recalls, "My partner and I got a call to go to what we thought was a domestic dispute. We went into the residence, and the noise was continuing while we were there. My partner asked the mother to please quiet her child, a boy who was on the floor with a kitchen chair on top of him. I remember that the parents were of a different ethnic background as I was collecting information, as my partner continually asked the mother to stop the boy from whining. The boy's father stood and watched, appearing oblivious to the situation. I was told by the boy's mother that 'things' were happening that they could not control. I asked her what these 'things' were that she was referring too. She pointed to the chair.

"At that point I kind of shook my head. My partner was getting somewhat impatient at that point and basically telling the kid to knock it off and ordering the parents to make him stop! To try and appease the mother, as well as my partner, I went to the boy and was going to lift the chair that was on top of him and stop this insanity. It was at that point I was like 'Wow!' The chair was literally glued or magnetized to the floor. It would not budge. I remember looking at my partner who gave me this 'look' like, 'What the heck?' I told him to come and try to lift the chair. Good luck with that one! He could not make it budge either! It was at that point we knew we had to re-evaluate the situation and truly listen to what the mother was telling us!

"It was not long after that the chair seemed to release its stuck-point to the floor. The boy was able to get free and stand up of his own accord. I was filling out the report in the kitchen area when I looked up just in time to see a plate come flying off a wall and just miss my head. My partner saw it too, and we just froze. 'What the hell!' My partner left and got out of there saying this was not a police matter. He actually muttered 'Leprechauns!' I soon followed his lead, telling the parents this was not a police matter, or at least one that we could handle. In my opinion, this was something that required further, more in depth investigation, and that is something that detectives do--detect!

"That was the last I ever was involved with that case. To be honest, it was one of those confusing, yet 'what the heck just happened?' moments one can experience. Whenever I am asked to recall how it 'felt' or what was going through my mind, I like to use the comparison to black ice. You are driving your vehicle in the winter, and all of a sudden you hit a patch of black ice. You start to spin out of control. You feel helpless. You can only hold on and do your best to steer in the direction of the slide. You can only hope you will be able to regain control and it will turn out fine. That was what that event will forever remind me of!"

Bob then discussed his "real" first moment which made him wonder what he had gotten himself into as a police officer investigating this case. "I remember sitting and talking to the parents, and I believe there were some friends of the family there as well," Bob recalled. "I was getting as many details as possible about what the heck was going on in the apartment when all of a sudden a chair just picked up and moved across the room. That wasn't the best part of it, oh no! The boy was sitting in the chair when it picked him up and took him across the room for ride. It made no sense as you are watching this!"

I asked Bob about the boy and if this happened often or if the boy was ever hurt by any of these uncanny, surreal events like the chair incidents. Bob shook his head confidently and answered, "Even when these things were happening to the boy, there were never any cuts or bruises on his body. It was one of the first things I looked for as well as asked the boy's parents."

You'd think with all that was going on there would be some sort of physical if not mental trauma going on with the boy. Bob stated that he thought the boy was handling the situation very well, showing no hysterics or discomfort. I asked Bob if he thought it was normal. Bob chuckled, "Normal? There was nothing normal about this case from the time that I walked in the apartment for the first time until the last time that I set foot in there and saw what was going on with the family. I will say this -- the boy handled things with dignity and was resilient (Author Peter Sacco's word choice). Nothing about this case had anything stable about it other than the lags of time between events--chaos in the apartment and then quiet.

"I witnessed many times the boy getting pushed against the wall or something else by some imaginary force that you couldn't see, but you knew it was there. Did I think the boy was play-acting and pretending that this 'pushing' was of his own doing? Absolutely not! I saw the force and suddenness with which he was being thrown into the walls. For his age, he would have had to been a good actor and looked quite surprised that this force would push him. There was no acting on the boy's part!"

I asked Bob if he saw others in the room at any time he was there including himself get pushed or have any incidents happen to them the same way things were happening to the boy. He shook his head. "For all of the times I responded to calls to the house or just popped in to check on the family, nothing happened to me. I always felt safe.

"There was one really interesting event which I did see which happened to another person present in the apartment. It actually surprised the heck out of the person and it involved a chair. I believe we had just been sitting in the kitchen. There was a priest present on this call. A friend of the family, I believe, called the priest to come or convinced the family to call. So there we were sitting in the kitchen talking with the priest who was getting information about what was going on in the apartment. The priest seemed to be open-minded about what was going on and didn't discount anything that was being described to him. I am guessing he was even more open-minded after he got up and witnessed what happened next to him!

"No sooner had he just finished asking the family questions that he got up and was going to go have a look around the apartment and, I think, interview the boy. That was when he turned his back, and the next thing I know is that the chair that the priest was sitting in seemed to fire itself, sliding across the floor, trying to trip the priest. He turned just in time and did not get bowled over."

I asked Bob how the priest reacted when he saw the projectile chair playing "bowling for priests?" He chuckled, somewhat bemused, and stated that the priest was not overly surprised. As he put it, "The priest almost appeared to be expecting something strange to happen." Bob asserted that the priest believed what was said to him without any cynicism, but kind of needed to see it for himself. And then when it did happen, there was a sense of satisfaction to proceed with whatever course of action he was planning to take. Bob said that this was only a teaser for the priest in terms of what he would be witnessing which I will be getting to later.

Bob told me that the mischievous and very annoying events continued to persist for the family. Bob stated that he was visiting the family regularly. The assaults, whatever they were, seemed only apparent when the young boy was around, and he was always the focal point. I will reiterate the point that Bob reassured that the boy was never harmed or traumatized by the continual happenings. In fact, he was "not horrified" in the least according to Bob. As I continued the interview with Bob, I asked him why he thought that was, or what he really thought was happening with all of this chaos and mayhem going on. Bob responded with one word, "Poltergeist!" He truly believed that this case was a poltergeist case, something psychokinetic being manifested by the boy and projected outward. He believed this to be the reason the boy was not being traumatized, and also the reason he never felt "scared" either.

As the noise in the building continually got worse and the police, namely Bob, was at the apartment quite often, it was time to bring in the reinforcements! According to Bob, a couple of detectives were there to see for themselves what in the hell was going on in the apartment. He recalls that they were there for a few hours interviewing the family (namely the boy), setting up tape recorders, and having their cameras ready. The entire time that they were there, much to their chagrin, nothing happened. They did not see or hear anything that had been discussed and documented to that point. They never went back. The same could not be said for the Crown attorney who visited the apartment!

Word got wind and made it to a Crown attorney who decided to see what was going on at the apartment for himself. He came to the apartment, Bob recalls, one late afternoon in February. He was seated with the entire family in the living room, along with Bob. "No sooner did he sit down and started to ask questions, the knocking started," Bob said. "And this is when the fun stuff started that would scare the hell out of him. You see, he asked about the banging sounds. He assumed it was the heater kicking in, you know, the old style water pipes. He was told by the family that the apartment building's heating system was checked by specialists (the gas company), and they were reassured there was nothing wrong with the pipes. In fact, it was only happening in the family's apartment--the knocking sounds, mostly in three's".

"He (the Crown attorney) appeared a little skeptical at that point, but that suddenly changed as the sounds grew louder! You see, the pictures on the wall started to move and shake...some crashed to the floor. He tried to make sense of what was going on, but nothing logical was coming to mind. Pictures continued to drop off of the wall, and some were almost coming off in a flying motion. You can imagine this was not too amusing for the Crown attorney as it was appearing to be overwhelming for him, and that is when a chair on its own, no one near it, suddenly went flying across the room in an upright position. It was almost as if this chair-moving event was just for him to see. He was not impressed in the least!

"I remember seeing the look on his face, not too pleasant. In fact, he was spooked to hell! He quickly got up and got the hell out of Dodge. He was so spooked, he left his brand new London Fog overcoat which he took off when he came in and never did come back for it!"

From that point onward, Bob stated that the "poltergeist" experiences, which he decided to call them continually, got worse and more intense. A couple of the more intense experiences happened before his very eyes. One of the more surreal one was when family and friends were seated in the living room on a couch. There were a few people sitting on the couch when it suddenly levitated upward on its own a foot off the floor before coming to a jarring bang. "Needless to say, the folks sitting on it that were not use to this sort of thing were a little shaken," Bob recalled. When you think about it, who the heck would ever get used to this sort of thing?

Bob went on to describe how "whatever force was at work" would torment the kid. In one instance, a shelf against the wall suddenly toppled over when the boy was putting on his winter coat and being taken away from the apartment. It was as if someone or something did not want him to leave. Furthermore, if that wasn't enough, one of his police cohorts witnessed the kid being tugged away from adults while he was sitting with them. Apparently, the boy was sitting on the lap of an adult and something was "trying to rip him away". A couple of officers tried to hold the kid down while this was all taking place. It was like something more than superhuman was trying to tug the kid away.

Many other smaller, yet "spooky," events continued to happen in which Bob discussed with me. One of the more intriguing ones was when a clock in the kitchen that they were looking at "just suddenly unplugged itself." In itself, if that was not disturbing enough, it got even better when the clock continued to pull itself off of the wall and then just set itself on the floor gently, as if placed there by a set of hands. "Things could be either destructive in that they would fall or crash, or you get these other kinds of events," Bob said.

Bob was once again adamant that this must have been a poltergeist, because all of these things only seemed to be happening when the boy was present. "It was as if it was only happening when he was around and because of him and for him." He cited that things would fall more often or become chaotic when only he was present. When he was at school, the mother reported nothing happened. In fact, when he was at school, nothing happened there either which was kind of interesting. Was there something about the apartment that set the boys "psychokinetic" powers off? Was there some "force" that existed only in the apartment that was in tune with the boy? After all, Bob mentioned that when the boy would walk past pictures, they would jiggle or move in unison, almost choreographed!

Bob then discussed "the major events" involving the bed! For all intents and purposes, this was what really made this case "famous" from what I learned about the case from police, professionals, as well as from the media and what they knew of it.

Bob recalled the event as follows, "We were sitting in the kitchen one evening talking to the parents. A priest was present. We were going over some of what was going on with the child when we heard noises coming from the boy's bedroom. We went to the room only to see, before our very eyes, the boy's bed levitating off of the floor with the child on it. The boy appeared frightened as he was sitting atop the bed looking at us helplessly. I believe the priest started to pray.

"I think I remember things moving around in the room as well as falling to the floor. The same was also happening in the apartment. There was a crucifix on the wall that remained intact where it was while everything else fell or flew to the floor. The child, who was getting very frightened, lunged off of the bed and came to his mother. While this was taking place, the bed, which was still in a suspended state of levitation, positioned itself atop two of the chairs that were in the room and rested a couple of feet off of the ground. It was the strangest thing I had ever seen!"

I asked Bob how things shaped up from a religious standpoint. "Did you or anyone else ask the priest what they thought it was--a possession or not?" The priest would not comment on it and would not say or use the word possession. The priest was considered a junior priest, and the family was a religious family of Catholic churchgoers," Bob stated. He did mention that sometime later he did believe that 'higher ups' from the church came to exercise the house!

I asked Bob when it all came to a head or a finish. When did police stop going and when were things basically ruled as 'complete' in all that the police could do? Bob stated it lasted for roughly the entire month of February. With that said, he said there were eleven days of absolute real mayhem which he considered to be the worst of what went on there. Bob mentioned that the occurrences in the apartment just appeared to stop, sometime around the visits from the priests. From that point forward, the police stopped going to the apartment, as did he. There were no other incidents that occurred after that one, in or around the area, and Bob asserted he knew of no others in the area.

The case, for all intents and purposes, was closed and more importantly he stated that the reports from the case were sealed for 6 or 8 years. He mentioned that while the mayhem was going on that February, reporters from all walks of life showed up trying to get exclusive stories. He said that the "biggest pain in the ass" was trying to protect the family and other tenants from the reporters. "You wanted to keep things dignified and private," Bob said. "It's got so bad that a couple of female reporters showed up wearing Roman Catholic nun costumes just to try and get inside for a look and talk to the family!"

Bob left me with a couple of salient points as we wrapped up our excellent interview. First, he wanted me to understand that as many decades as he had been a police officer, he had never seen anything like this case ever, or anywhere else. "I never heard of any other cops working these types of cases," he said. Secondly, I asked him how seriously the circumstances surrounding this case were taken by his fellow cops and other professionals associated with it? "Very seriously!" he said. "This was not one of those cases one took lightly or laughed about!"

The family moved out of their apartment for a short time to stay with relatives. While they were with their relatives, there were no reported incidents or disturbances. Eventually, they would return to the apartment, and thereafter there were no more disturbances. At the end of the day, was it a poltergeist, a possession, or a haunting? If it were a poltergeist, why didn't it occur in other locations whenever the boy was present? If it was a haunting, why did the "haunted stuff" not start back up when they returned? If it were a poltergeist, tied to the apartment only and triggered/stimulated back into existence when the boy was present, why did it not start up again? And what did the priests do--an exorcism? Is this why the chaos, mayhem, or haunting going-ons finally stopped? These are interesting questions that have not been fully or nearly answered, for that matter, to this day.

This case was so interesting, exciting, and dare I say "entertaining" that it made headlines around the world. I read somewhere that even Johnny Carson, the great former host of the Tonight Show, mentioned it during his show!

CASES OF THE MYSTERIOUS AND MACABRE

Copy of Police Report from 1970 Poltergeist Case--Courtesy of Bob "Scotty Crawford

KEY POINTS FROM THIS CASE

* There were never any foul or obnoxious odors.

* There was knocking on the walls, usually in "three's".

* Both small objects (pictures, clocks, papers, etc.) along with large objects (shelves/book cases, chairs, sofas, and beds) moved on their own or levitated.

* There were no dramatic shifts in temperature, neither hot nor cold.

* There were never any visible apparitions or shadows present.

* There were priests present, but they never commented on the events going on.

* Apparently, after one of the last visits by a priest, the events suddenly stopped.

CHAPTER TWO

AN EVIL HAUNTED HOUSE

Thirteen years ago, go figure -- the number 13 comes into play in this story, a couple of people came to me to discuss a haunted house. At the time, I was working on a production entitled *Haunted Niagara*, a one hour documentary that was to be a featured show for Halloween. Interestingly, the show would go on to become so popular that no matter where I went in the Niagara Region, someone would comment on the show and how much they loved it, before telling me their own ghost or haunted story. This time, this story was a little different that these folks shared with me. They were, let me just say, very convincing and they "spooked" me actually!

For the purpose of this chapter, I have chosen not to divulge where this house is located in terms of its location (city or address). I will say this much, it is between the USA/Canadian border of Fort Erie and Centennial Parkway in Stoney Creek, Ontario. How is that for stretching the Niagara Region out to its fullest length and breadth? With that said, the house truly does exist and someone lives in it part-time...sort of. You see, according to legend, rumour has it, that a family once lived in this rather large house before the bank took the house over when the family stopped making payments on the house after they left it, and a new owner took possession of the house and has had it ever since -- say at least a few decades now. Getting back to the family...

I was given a brief history of the home by the folks I mentioned previously. It was one afternoon midweek when I sauntered into a popular coffee shop when this couple recognized me from *Haunted Niagara* as they had been in Niagara Falls at one of the indoor water parks and caught it on TV. They asked if I would join them and, as they put it, "pick my brain." I always thought that analogy is just a little too close to something from a George Romero film, or now more mainstream, *The Walking Dead*! Needless to say, they sequestered me and hit me with a ton of questions about the documentary and anything that I might have seen that I never covered in the production. That is when they eluded to "the house". They informed me of "this house" that had a part-time owner in it, or as they affectionately put it, "a caretaker that was there to protect the house." I listened intently. They asked me if

I thought that a house could be purely evil. That was an interesting question as my mind momentarily shifted to the exceptional Stephen King book *Salem's Lot*, which scared the hell out of me as a kid! I will never forget the character Ben Mears asking one of the main characters in the book if he thought a house on its own could be purely evil. Ironically, Ben Mears was an author inquiring about scary houses like yours truly! Sipping on my coffee, which was actually kicking my mind into another gear, I continued to listen to them.

"The family just up and left in the middle of the night!" one of the ladies told me.

"Just left? What do you mean? Did they leave the house in the middle of the night because something scared them?" I asked.

"Yes, they left in the middle of the night and did not come back...ever!" she responded.

What I was told was that a family lived in this very old house, a home well over a hundred years old. Something spooked the hell out of them enough to make them just leave and without packing up their belongings. Supposedly, they never went back to the house. I heard, from other sources, similar stories along this line, with some ascertaining that the family did send for their belongings. Conversely, I also heard from one reputable source who spoke to a friend who is familiar with the going-ons at that house for several decades that nothing that dramatic ever happened. Was there really some kind of ghost, apparition, poltergeist, or demon that scared them away from the house -- if that is in fact what had really happened? Did we have something similar to the Amityville Horror story going on within the Niagara Region?

The folks who told me about the family abandoning the house continued to tell me more. The kicker was what one of the ladies told me next.

"My niece, who is in her early twenties, and a couple of her friends decided, against their better judgement, to worm their way into the house through one of the boarded up windows one weekend late at night. One of her friends had this brilliant idea to communicate with the spirits or ghosts of the house. This friend of my niece was into taboo stuff, well at least in my books, that had to do with the occult. She brought with her Tarot cards, some candles, and some other paraphernalia hoping to conjure up the spirits and communicate with them.

"I was told by the girls it was a cold night, so the basement where they got in was damp and musky-smelling, and there was no shortage of dust. As advertised, the house was completely derelict--no furniture in the basement. The basement would be the only room they would see for all intents and purposes! The girls were not in the house for more than ten minutes before they had the candles going and the cards laid out on the floor. Suddenly, the cards caught fire and went quickly up in flames. The girls immediately bolted from the house!"

I asked these folks telling me the story if the girls ever went back into the house, and I was told, "No way!" If what they said really happened, then I sure as heck wouldn't blame them!

The girls were quite shaken up by the event with the burning cards, but also would not have been able to get into the house because, not too long after, the house was being lived in and was refurbished and refurnished so to speak.

The first time I had ever been to the house to see it myself, I thought it was pretty creepy. There was no denying the fact that it was the type of house written about in horror novels, the kind that would appear to be haunted, and a type of house which could quickly become the setting of urban legends. I saw the house both before and after it was being lived in. When it was derelict, I could see how some people, especially ghost hunters, could be fascinated by it and inclined to want to go inside it and see what was inside. Even with it being lived in "part-time," so I was told, I could see how stories of the paranormal might still surround the house. There was still a lot more to this house. Let me explain...

A very good and dear friend of mine, who passed away in the mid 2000's, was a clairvoyant/psychic. When I refer to her that way, I do so with the utmost respect and admiration--she was the real deal! She was so good, that police services would show up on her doorstep, often times unannounced, to get help with leads on cases involving missing people and murders. She told me that sometimes the police services would be from other parts of the world outside of Canada. For the record, I am a skeptic when it comes to this kind of stuff (psychics, clairvoyants, and seers). We were friends for a while before she told me "stuff" about my life. When I refer to "stuff," I'm talking about things from my past that I had never told anyone. She even named names, as well as stated to me when certain people would show back up in my life. She was right! I didn't know how the heck she did it, but she made a believer out of me even though I would probe her for answers as to "how". She would always tell me that she didn't know how, that it was just a "gift" she had since childhood. The reason I bring my friend up is because I trust in her and her abilities. She was also fascinated by ghost stories and haunted places, so I thought she would find this house fascinating.

The folks that told me stories about the house had handed me a few pictures of the place and some shots of the neighbouring properties. I brought the pictures to my friend's house, and we had lunch together, along with her husband. I showed her the pictures. She was enthralled by them!

According to her, there was "something definitely not right" about the house. She got a bad feeling from it. In fact, she asserted that it was a bad place. Being the adventurer that I am, she quickly made me promise her that I would never set foot inside the house. She told me that I would not be going into the house for two reasons. First off, she didn't think that the house was safe in terms of structure. She "saw" the potential for someone to fall through rotted floor boards. Second, she asserted that the place did have something sinister about it and staying out was one's best measure. I should also point out that these pictures and our conversation were taking place while the house was still empty with no one living in it.

She wanted me to show it to some other people who had psychic abilities, people she did not know. She was curious to know what they had to say about the house. The first fellow I met was a dowser--one who has the ability to locate water, minerals, or noxious gas under the ground using a divining rod. This is what this fellow did for a living after retiring from his 9-5 job. I learned that he was able to find negative energies in homes using his divining rod and pendulum. The negative energies that I am referring to here are bad spirits, according to his claims. He referred to them as toxic and noxious spirits. When I asked this gentleman if he meant that the "spirits" were intelligent (humanistic-origin spirits), he stated that they were and that they had once been living humans in the house and had died in the house.

He told me that he had been watching that particular house for some time. What he told me, at the time, made me wonder how realistic -- not to mention sane -- his claims were. He told me the spirits were those of teenagers, males to be exact, that would taunt him whenever he was around the house. With that said, I asked him what the teenage spirits wanted. Joking, I quoted the Nirvana song, "Smells Like Teen Spirit." He didn't get my sarcasm. He wasn't into Nirvana! Seriously, what he did state was that these spirits wanted to leave the dwelling. He told me that they were stuck there and if they could attach themselves to someone living, they would be going for a car ride with whoever would play chauffer to them. Furthermore, he claimed that if they could truly follow one home, they would take up residency in the new host's house. Great--a house full of teenagers I thought!

I listened to his assessment of the house and its history – that is the history he had with it as he did not know it's true history -- and went away thinking, "Cool story, another urban legend!" It was only after meeting these folks who had told me about the burning Tarot cards that

I recalled what the dowser told me and sort of rethought things, you know the kind of stuff that makes you go "Hmmmmmm!" Indeed, things had become a little more telling!

According to these folks that were sharing their stories about the house, I quickly learned that the house, nearly 100 years ago, had been a hostel/foster home for troubled youth as well as immigrants. The majority of those living in the home, at any given time, were teenage males. With that said, one of the gentlemen told me, that as far back as he could remember, a teenage male had killed another teen in the house. Facing stiff punishment from the authorities back in the day, the killer decided to take his own life and hanged himself in the house. As he was telling me bits and pieces of this story, my mind kept shifting back to what the dowser had told me. The words, "One of the boys is very bad, a sociopath..." kept ringing in my head. The people describing the house continued to tell me their stories. When they were done, I asked them about dowsing. The best they could tell me about it is what they saw in movies or TV where people were trying to find water or gold using divining rods. When I asked them if they had heard about using divining rods to find spirits, they looked at me like I had three eyes. The reason I asked was because I wanted to know if they knew the dowser gent or heard of him to discern whether they were in cahoots with their stories. They weren't! Therefore, there was a consistency to the story of the house based on two different sources, neither party knowing the other. Then it was time to call in the big guns...

Enter a psychic/clairvoyant! I called upon someone I know who has psychic abilities. He is not your everyday psychic either. He is from the USA and was visiting Canada for a couple of weeks. Through a friend, I was able to pose an interesting proposition to him, "If I brought you to a house, would you be able to tell me stuff about it?" This psychic is very gifted and always up for a challenge. In this case I was kind of playing coy and pretending I knew next to nothing about the house and asked if he could help me out. It took a couple of days for him to agree, but he eventually went along with the challenge.

It was toward the end of last summer (2012) when we visited the house. There were a few of us that went, and my intention was for us to observe it from afar -- meaning from across the street inconspicuously from my SUV. When we got to the house and I parked the car, he was instantly enthralled by it. You'd swear someone just lit the candles on his birthday cake, and he was going to blow them out! Instantly, he and his wife bolted from my vehicle and ran to the house. *Great!* I thought. All I needed were cousins Clem and Cletus to come out of the house holding double-barreled shotguns saying, "Can I help you, boy?"

I could not believe my eyes! He literally ran to the house and started "feeling" it! He would later tell me he felt it to feel its energy and to understand what was going on in the house. I drove down the street and hid behind some trees and shrubs where I couldn't see him. I waited for what seemed like an eternity with a friend. We started our own pool of what would happen first -- yelling sounds coming from the owner of the house or seeing police lights in the rear view mirror. Neither happened, as mercifully his "feeling session" with the house ended and he returned to the vehicle just as I was going to send out the search party...myself.

As he and his wife got in, I drove away rather quickly, speeding off into the dark night. There was a long moment of silence in the SUV. I could hear the seatbelt warning beeping as neither they nor myself still did not have our seatbelts on. In unison, we put them on, and I glanced at him in the rear view mirror. Our eyes locked on one another and he smirked. "Are you ready to hear what I have to say, my friend?" he asked.

I will reiterate -- he knew nothing about this house and very little about the location we were at other than the name of the city. He proceeded to tell us about the bad and negative energy that was at the house. He went on for about five minutes discussing this as well the negative spirits that were still there and have been there for a long time. It was then I asked, "What kind of spirits are there?"

His response was as follows, "There are not-so-pleasant spirits in the house that are restless, angry...perhaps violent. I sensed that the spirits are those of teenagers...boys to be more exact. Something tragic happened in the house many years ago. One died in the house and is very angry. That was what I got." He went on to describe other things about the house, nothing about a family leaving it, or anything like that, but more superficial things. I was pleasantly surprised that he had described the teenage spirits, this after more than a decade since the dowser had described them, and not long after the folks who told me about the house described the correlation to teenagers. For someone who had never been to the area, he pretty much verified what others had told me.

Can a house be haunted? It seems we read about them all of the time and there are a throng of TV shows which investigate haunted houses. The more interesting question is, "Can a house be evil or contain evil?" According to those who told me about the house, all said, "Yes!"

Interestingly, as this book is about to go to publication, I was in the area where this "haunted house" is yesterday. I learned from another source a new family has just bought the house and is moving in as I type this!

KEY POINTS FROM THIS CASE

* Several people who did not know one another had similar experiences or heard about them with regards to this house.

* Several different psychics and mediums reported having similar "feelings" and/or visions about the house.

* There is no definitive history on the stories or psychic assertions that can be verified.

CHAPTER THREE

HAUNTED TREES AND FORESTS

I am sure you have probably read or heard about fairy tales containing stories of enchanted forests. Perhaps you have heard similar stories of darker, more sinister stories such as the Black Forest. When it comes to the premise of haunted forests, whenever they are mentioned or discussed in literature or paranormal investigations, they always possess some sinister component to them, components that are independent of the naturally-occurring wildlife.

There is the old adage, "If a tree falls in a forest, does it make a sound if no one is around to hear the sound?" The answer is obviously a philosophical one, but the real question perhaps should be, "What made the tree fall in the first place?" Of course, that is, if you believe in the paranormal!

Haunted forests have gotten some pretty interesting attention in literature and in the media. I looked into why a haunted forest would or could become so popular in media, and I had some pretty interesting findings. Of course, one of the biggies, when it comes to explaining haunted forests, is the correlations to Bigfoot or Sasquatch -- you know the hairy, giant, ape-like creatures that roam the woods, undetected, and unfound? Yes, there are many who believe haunted forests are being harbored by these ape-like creatures which make them appear paranormal.

Then, there was the fairy-like explanation. Whether it is a Snow White-based ideology or even like the TV series *TrueBlood* for that matter, some people believe that forests are the places for make-believe -- you know the enchanted place where fairies fly flicking their pixie dust on unsuspecting travelers and where animals talk! It's not the greatest or most feasible explanation, is it? In fact, if you want to believe in haunted forests, then this explanation is an obvious downer-- nothing too scary about pixie dust!

This then leads to another explanation and one that has garnered more interest. What if forests were doorways or gateways to parallel universes...wormholes? *Wormhole* you might be asking? I am not referring to tiny, narrow passages created by the creepy-crawlers that come out at night when the soil is moist. I am referring to the theoretical passageways that some believe exist in the universe which allow for overcoming the space-time continuum making time travel infinitely possible. Without getting all scientific here and into quantum physics, let's just say some believe in the ability to really go *Back to the Future* without needing a stainless steel-bodied Delorean!

When it comes to parallel universes, some "experts", whoever they might be believe that these wormholes connect us and get us to said parallel universes. What is a parallel universe exactly? It's another universe exactly like the one we live in or related to ours where other humans and animals exist. Some even believe there are doppelgangers of ourselves (our twins or another version of ourselves) that exist there. Some of you reading this are probably thinking, *Gee, can we go back to option number two with the fairies and talking animals?*

What if parallel universes did exist and forests were indeed the gateways? The rationale for the possibility of this, some would assert since there is so much space plus no urban development, could make this the prime location for these gateways or habitats to exist. In fact, some believe that open fields, prairies of land, are even better! Could these parallel universes --wormholes -- really exist? If so, is there any validity to forests being haunted in this way? Are there folks from other universes or dimensions lurking in the forests? My aim was to find out a little more about these haunted forests, more so in the Niagara Region.

I personally, with the help of some friends, decided to hike through some of the more popular forests in the Niagara Region, namely the Bruce Trail as well as the Short Hills. What was I looking for? I don't know! I would see for myself if there was anything weird, mysterious, or haunted going on in these forests.

CASES OF THE MYSTERIOUS AND MACABRE

Do trees have "haunted" spirits or powers? A tree I came across on one of my hikes.

I guess for starters, enquiring minds, namely my mind, wanted to know what would qualify making a forest being haunted. I was given two repeated answers: the deafening silence and the sense of constantly being watched. These were the two intangibles. Then there was the tangible answer, stated many times...the trees! Okay so, let's start with the silence, since after all, do they not say silence is golden?

Most people assert that they love the forests and trails for hiking because, to quote the great band Depeche Mode, they "enjoy the silence!" You see, they are naturists, so the beauty and sounds of nature make sense to them. They find nothing spooky or daunting about the silence of the forest. Conversely, it was the people whom I spoke with who rarely hike or spend time in the forest that found the sounds most disturbing. They quoted the quiet forest as being ominous in terms of sound. They were used to hearing man-made sounds of nature, and most claimed those sounds provided a sense of comfort to them. What it truly meant is they never felt alone! In a nutshell, the sounds of the forest, or lack of man-made sounds made them feel alone. Moreover, to feel or be alone was a scary prospect to them. Some even asserted that when there is forest silence, only the sounds of nature, you hear things that you are not used to hearing, or you imagine hearing things and this scares the hell out of you!" So much for silence being golden for some! On my own hiking experiences, I did hear the naturally occurring sounds of birds, insects, brooks, waterfalls, squirrels, snakes slithering across the terrain, and the wind rustling through the leaves of trees, and not once did I feel afraid. With that said, I could swear I did hear these imaginary sounds they were talking about. That only occurred once after I was lost for about an hour in the forest on one of my hikes. I wasn't afraid of the imaginary sounds, except for maybe a little, when I considered daylight was quickly dissipating and I was in the middle of a forest...lost!

The second fearful component people reported about forests was the feeling of being watched. I can only say I felt at times I was being watched by birds and other critters, but not by human eyes standing in the doorway of a parallel universe or eyes belonging to a forest phantom or fairies. I will say this much however, one of the ladies on our excursion reported several times feeling as if we were being watched or followed. Before the group of us set out on our hike and during it, not once did I mention anything about going through a potentially haunted forest or expecting to see anything paranormal or describing anything of the sort. Interestingly, this lady asserted she was feeling as if creepy eyes were watching her. Of course this produced a ripple effect or contagious effect for others on the hike. Since she kept reporting it, others then started to not only feel eyes upon them, but of course they started to hear the imaginary sounds. I seized this as my opportunity to mention that some forests are known to be haunted, and some people have reported that this one trail we were on has had some ties to the paranormal. Instantly, all bets were off for everyone being a skeptic! I had more folks starting to feel creeped out and some actually wanting to leave as they worried we might become abducted. When I asked who they thought would abduct us, I was told "the Trees!" Of course, it all made sense now...the trees were the culprits!

Do forests really possess some kind of magic? Short hills in St. Catharines, Ontario at dusk.

Speaking of the trees, I have had people tell me legends that had been passed down through the generations about trees being haunted. In mythology, trees took on a persona of mystery, one in which they were a bewitching part of nature. The Druids used trees as places of gathering for worship. They never worshipped the trees, which some believed to be the case. Moreover, other pagan groups were known to worship trees. Did they believe them to possess some sort of magical essence? It is funny how many people I spoke with discussed their fascination with trees. Some asserted that trees are beautiful for the most part, but when trees were in their natural environment (the forest), they took on a whole new life so to speak. There were folks who believed that trees actually communicate with one another (Their branches come to life like arms, and their roots can purposely trip you up.), and that they can actually move as if to purposely make a hiker get lost.

It was more so the types of trees which both fascinated and frightened most. Weeping willows, no surprise, perhaps due to their loping, slithering branches, held the greatest apprehension for some who were frightened by trees. Others claimed it were conifer trees (pine, spruce, etc.) that they found more intimidating because they were winter trees, and the thought of being alone in a winter forest was lonely and frightening. I wanted to get back to my initial point of investigation by doing this hike with others, asking those I knew who hiked a lot and people in general, "Were there such things as haunted forests, and if so, did they exist in the Niagara Region?"

It seemed that several people I spoke with did report feelings of "awe", the "uncanny" and even "spooky" when it came to places like the Bruce Trail, the Short Hills, and also DeCew Falls. I had some people believe that they truly saw things moving in the forest, things larger than small animals, critters, and birds. They appeared to be there one moment and then gone the next. Also, some folks also claimed that the trees that they swore they used as markers on their hikes had shifted spots, no longer where they once were. "It was if the trees were playing tricks on us!" a couple of hikers told me.

At the end of the day, if you are a hiker and you believe in haunted places, then perhaps a nice long hike into a wonderland of trees will provide you with more than you bargained for. Perhaps you might get so lost, that you disappear and are never heard from again. Then again, you might be calling from a parallel universe, but we are just not able to hear you!

KEY POINTS FROM THIS CASE

* Some experts from different branches of science/quasi-sciences believe in the existence of parallel universes.

* Some paranormal experts believe that forests and prairies/fields are where doorways or gateways exist to enter other universes.

* Some paranormal investigators and witnesses believe that trees/forests possess lives of their own beyond natural laws.

CHAPTER FOUR

ORBS AT DECEW FALLS

In the last chapter story, I mentioned DeCew Falls. I thought this chapter would be a great place to continue on DeCew Falls and the haunted stories surrounding it.

I set out with my team of four to check out DeCew Falls. I had heard stories about an apparition haunting the old mine shaft midway up to the right of the largest Falls. There are three waterfalls in all at DeCew Falls.

I had never been to DeCew Falls, that is at the base of it, ever in my life. It is actually not that easy to get to I might add! We started out from the street and made our way through the forest, at times using one of my colleague's GPS on his cell phone. Okay, we cheated, but it wouldn't be cool to get lost in there, especially with a hundred pounds of camera equipment we were lugging with us to film *Niagara's Most Haunted*. By the way, remember the last chapter focused on haunted forests? Perhaps this wouldn't be a great place to be after dark. The mosquitoes were killers, so we were armed with bug spray!

The forest hike was very daunting to say the least. It is not easy getting around the river bank as the rocks are very slippery, and there are times where you literally have to scale the edge of the embankments (actually there are some ropes tied to trees and cliffs) just to make it around and past the first of the waterfalls. The first waterfalls are stunning! We got to see it in mid-summer, and the cool mist was very refreshing for a very sticky, early evening. There were no mentions of ghosts at this waterfall, so we proceeded to the other two which are found side by side.

The main waterfall and the one next to it are exceptional. The view from the bottom was breathtaking! We made our way up as we watched the last of the swimmers, who had been playing in the basin of the waterfall, leave. The water in the basin is a very dark, algae-tainted green, probably not the best for swimming and definitely not drinkable!

Scaling the hill to get to the midpoint was no easy task. You see, a couple of weeks prior, the Niagara Region got hit with one heck of a major rainstorm following two weeks of intense heat and humidity. (Ironically, we had come to DeCew Falls two weeks earlier and cancelled our hike 1/4 of the way through as it was way too hot!). The rainwater had seeped into the mud making it still very slick. This time we scaled the hill using branches and plant chutes jetting out from the ground. One of my team members who was wearing a GoPro camera on his head went for a spill as he was trying to make it down from one of these hills to another one. It was not a pretty sight. We were lucky there were no casualties!

DeCew Falls itself is rich in history. The main falls is seventy-two feet high, cascading into an amazing bowl-shaped basin. The roar of the falls is trapped within the amphitheatre-like setting. The basin-shaped pond begins to run off into the creek which winds for miles.

At the top of the falls is an old stone mill. It was built in 1872 for blacksmithing and carpentry. It is in excellent shape as it was rebuilt after being destroyed in a fire in 1895. From what I was able to find, there were no casualties and it is not known to be haunted. It now serves as a museum.

The mine shaft at the base of DeCew Falls was supposedly operational through the 1800's from what information I could find. The mine was used as a water tunnel by the DeCew Power Company back in the day to discharge water from the turbines. From what I was able to dig up information-wise, I never came across any deaths or accidents associated with the use of the mine in the past when it was in operation or to this very day. Were there really ghosts in the mine? Was it really haunted?

Old mill at DeCew Falls 2013.

My team and I hiked inside of the mine when we were half way up the stone embankment. Instantly, there was a temperature drop as we set foot in the cold, damp, musky smelling mine shaft. The bottom of the mine was flooded with about a foot of water, so we used the rocks on the ground as steps until we made it to the old train track which was pretty rusty and slippery. There was also a lot of mist blowing from the large DeCew Falls and making its way into the mine shaft making it even more slippery for walking. With that said, the tunnel itself had a certain mystique to it--dreary, yet alive, cozy, yet scary...at least in the darkness!

What were we hoping to see besides filming for the TV show? Rumour or legend had it that there were apparitions that roamed inside the mine shaft. In the past, hikers have reported seeing people, which they would later deduce to be apparitions, walk inside of the tunnel and disappear. When we were inside the entrance of the mine shaft, we could only go in so far, as the tunnel is then locked off by a large, thick, metal gate. So were these people who saw these apparitions confused, assuming that they disappeared into thin air? After all, the gate was not always there, so is it safe to say they were other hikers just going into the tunnel and checking things out for themselves? Okay, let's put things in perspective...

Peter Sacco standing at the base of the first of the 3 falls at DeCew.

The tunnel itself, I learned, when it was open past the now locked iron gate was nearly 500 metres long. It does come to an end for those who are able to walk it if and when the gate was open. From what I was told, if you did walk through the tunnel, you would come to large pipes and wood which sort of seal it. If that isn't enough there is a large steel plate at the end. I also Googled the tunnel to find what I could on the subject and basically found the same information...no way out! So, if these were indeed other hikers, where did they go? They would not have been able to make it out through the other side if it were blocked off, right? And from what I was able to learn about the mine shaft, there were no other exits along the way. Were these then indeed apparitions?

Taping in mine shaft for episode of Niagara's Most Haunted 2013. Notice the orbs created by mist droplets.

    I dug deeper, no not through the mine, but rather through research to find out what I could about these apparitions. The best I could find were that most of these apparitions had been reported by university and college students attending close-by schools who apparently witnessed seeing them. Perhaps this all came down to perception, the time of day, and who had what and how much to drink! Let's face it -- many urban legends and ghost stories are started by teens/youth at night. This is a great place for teens to party from what I was told. In fact, we saw enough litter (bottles, wrappers, etc) on our walk along the creek to get to the various falls which would support this. Could there be other types of spirits present?

Gate leading into the mine shaft tunnel that is locked to keep hikers out.

While doing research, I was told by some people I spoke with that orbs often appear in photos that people have taken by DeCew Falls and the mine shaft. Some people believe that orbs are spirits caught on film. Were these the spirits people believed they were catching on film inside of the mine shaft? I never heard that these orbs were trying to communicate with anyone. They just showed up in photos.

We did a fair bit of camera work both around and inside the mine shaft. We used both still cameras as well as motion picture cameras. I can tell you that we saw nothing with the naked eye in terms of orbs. However, when we started shooting with still cameras, wowser! There were orbs everywhere!

It was easy to figure out where these orbs were coming from. The sun was now setting behind us. With that said, the light of the sun was bouncing off the mist and beads of water in the mine shaft. It was safe to say that the orbs we were seeing were more of a by-product of light bouncing off beads of water. There was nothing sinister or paranormal about these orbs we were seeking. This is not to say there are not orbs in the tunnel other than the ones being manufactured by nature through water plus sunlight!

I can honestly say there was nothing haunting about the various falls or the mine shaft. I will say this however...If you look through the locked gate in the mine shaft and stare into it as the sun is setting, there is a distinct mist, perhaps caused by the humidity which can definitely play tricks with your eyes when you shine a flash light into it. Perhaps this was and still is the apparitions folks are seeing--cloudy, misty reflections of light, perhaps even reflections of our own vivid imaginations.

Peter Sacco standing in front of main falls at DeCew Falls 2013.

One other interesting tidbit of information--DeCew Falls was the place Laura Secord set as the destination of her famous walk back in June of 1813. Secord set out on her famous trek to warn the British that the Americans were coming to attack them. She walked from what is now the town of Queenston through the Niagara Escarpment to get to the famous DeCew House to warn the British. The ruins of the DeCew House remain today with a variety of plaques and landmarks commemorating her mission. Some folks have also reported seeing the apparitions or hearing screams of soldiers from the War of 1812 late in the evenings at this site.

CASES OF THE MYSTERIOUS AND MACABRE

Ruins of the DeCew House (built by John DeCou, now called DeCew House)--Laura Secord made her famous walk here from Queenston Heights during War of 1812.

KEY POINTS FROM THIS CASE

* Folks on many occasions reports seeing orbs or capturing them on photos in the old mine shaft.

*Some people, namely teens, have reported seeing an apparition disappear in the tunnel of the old mine shaft.

* Historically, there were no tragedies or traumatic events that occurred at DeCew Falls which would lead to ghosts or apparitions haunting the area.

*The ruins of the DeCew House remain--the end destination of Laura Secord's famous trek to warn the British Army in the War of 1812.

CHAPTER FIVE

DO PHANTOMS REALLY EXIST?

I had heard similar stories in the past, but to hear it again kind of made the hair on the back of my neck stand up. In fact, it made my skin crawl thinking that this could actually happen!

After I had just completed a lecture, there were a handful of people standing at the podium waiting to talk to me. A fellow wearing a grey fedora asked if I had some time to join him along with the ladies he was with for coffee. He promised me that the story I was about to hear was definitely worth my time and the coffee and dessert they were about to buy me. Did someone say free coffee and dessert?

Author Peter Sacco's rendition of what many people believe a phantom to look like.

As we sat in the cafe, I listened as the lady, who told me that she was in her late 30's, began to tell her story. "It happened two years ago," she began. "I had just moved here from Alberta. The lady sitting next to me is my older sister, and she asked me to come and live with her as I had just taken a buyout from the chain of stores I was working for. I had visited the Niagara Region in the past, so I knew I liked it and wouldn't mind living here.

"Within three months of moving here, my brother-in-law (pointing to the fellow who was wearing the fedora) was able to get me a job at a printing company. I am mostly at the front desk when you walk in. I have full view people as they walk in and out. That was when I noticed a fellow who was always in the store looking at things and staring at me. This went on for a good couple of weeks. He would be in at least 3-4 times a week. He would occasionally speak to one of the fellows who works in the store and I believe he finally placed an order for a job when I was not there. He was a good looking guy, but he was really creepy, if you know what I mean.

"The guy always wore a black pinstriped sports coat with either grey or black pants and always had a silk handkerchief in the breast pocket. Don't get me wrong. He was always very well-dressed and a good looking man, distinguished, with kind of salt and pepper hair. The way he just stared at me was the creepy part of it I guess. It was like his eyes would look right through me. I would smile sheepishly if and when I caught him staring, and he would always smile back at me.

"Around the third week of seeing him in the store, he actually came to the counter when I was alone and introduced himself and said hi. I was kind of taken off guard as I didn't think he would actually talk to me, but before I knew it I was exchanging pleasantries with him. It was actually nice. He was very nice, and I found him even better looking up close the more he spoke. We made small talk, mostly about the area where I moved from and travel. He said he loved to travel and started telling me about a trip to Europe he planned in the fall. The more he talked to me, the more I found him enthralling, if you call it that. He had peaked my interest as he seemed to say all of the right things!

"Before I knew it, I was doing something I had never thought I would have imagined doing when I first laid eyes on this fellow. I agreed to go to dinner with him. Dinner was at a very nice restaurant in Niagara on the Lake. He spared no costs as we ate and drank one of the finest bottles of wine, living like royalty. We stayed at the restaurant for what was at least a few hours, and I don't know if my inhibitions were down because of the wine I had drank, but he asked me to go back to his place to 'chill' as he put it. I agreed too easily!

"My time spent at his place was definitely not what I expected! I was a little worried about him putting the moves on me as we drove to his place which was about a half hour away from the restaurant, but that didn't happen. In fact, there were no moves, rather a movie. Furthermore, he asked me to watch the movie alone while he got up many times to disappear into the kitchen or bathroom. It was weird to say the least, but he made sure my glass of wine, which he served me, was always refreshed. He reassured me that I probably would not be spending the night, unless I really wanted to, and that he would drive me home. So, I watched the movie and drank away. Interestingly, the movie was a vampire movie, one I had never seen before, perhaps an older one which came from Europe.

"The movie stunk to be blunt. It was silly at best, and I found myself laughing several times, actually at the scenes in it which were supposed to be serious I think. My date did not look too amused at my laughter and less amused when he asked me after the movie what I thought about it. I was very tipsy and giddy, so of course I was not taking anything too serious. I told him I thought the movie was for kiddies--silly for a more better term. At that comment, I will never forget the look in his eyes as he glared at me and then sat across from me in his leather chair. By the way, his house, an old brownstone, was decorated in very dark-coloured furniture, velvet borders, and of course several antiques. The large screen TV was definitely no antique!

"His eyes...those eyes...they cut through me like laser beams. I felt like a school girl getting in trouble for passing a note in class while the teacher was speaking. Just as sudden as his furrowed gaze targeted me, it dissipated into a greasy smile, which is the best way to describe it as his lips slowly parted. There was zero attractiveness about this man in that moment. In fact, he was downright creepy-ugly if there is such a word! He slowly studied my expressions and cleared his throat, saying my name slowly and methodically three times...

"*'Do you know who I am?'* he asked. Was this some kind of loaded question? I didn't know what to say to that or how to answer. I only knew what he had told me. He was of European descent, had a company through which he imported things into Canada, was never married, and had no kids. Oh yes, he was also at least ten years older than I was. Jokingly, I mused, *'You're a movie critic?'* He chuckled and then asked me how long had we known each other. I said maybe a month. He chuckled again and then asked me if I forgot all about him.

"Nothing was registering at that point. I had no idea what he was talking about until he started describing the house I lived in back in the early 1980's with my mother, sister, and step-father. In fact, he described them all to a tee—which was disturbing as hell! How could he have known all of these details? Some were too intimate for me to get into or describe, but he knew me as a teenager...IMPOSSIBLE!

"He proceeded to tell me more. I stirred in the large, soft brown, leather sofa I was seated in. It seemed to amuse him more and more with each tidbit of information he shared with me. *'How?'* I kept asking him. He would just smile and proceed onto something else or some other intimate detail. Finally...something clicked! I remembered something which sent ripples down the back of my neck before evolving to shock waves throughout my entire body. The bastard really knew who I was and all about me because he had once seen me as a teenager and now I had remembered him. Only something was wrong! You know when you have that déjà vu feeling moment where you feel like you've lived something before and it is unfolding for you in the present? Only at this present moment, the feelings were quite intense--off the map intense! The only thing I could force out of my mouth was, *'How ... you haven't changed...at all!'*

"First off, this is 2010. I am seeing this guy in the real now moment, okay, like me sitting on his couch. I first and did see him in the early 1980's. I am a teenager then, I think sixteen years old. I am also living in Alberta in a farmhouse. This is the Niagara region I am in now. And here is this guy I first saw in the 1980's in my house, my bedroom to be exact, who looks the exact same. There was no doubt it was him. I know you probably think I am definitely crazy, had too much wine to drink, but he started it...he was the one who brought this discussion up and filled in all of the details. It was as real for him as it was for me, so what the hell? I was scared, but more curious sitting across from him in that moment.

"In the 1980's I remember sitting in my bedroom one night reading as I couldn't sleep. I had the night light on next to my bed as I was reading. Out of the corner of my eye I could swear I saw something move. I thought it was my tired eyes playing tricks on me. At first I didn't look up, but then when I did, I saw *HIM*! This guy was sitting on a bean-bag chair off in the corner of my room next to the closet. I was horrified! I was reading a Stephen King book, so I thought I was semi-asleep and put the book down. As I rubbed my eyes, looking up again expecting to see an empty space on the bean-bag chair, there HE was, still sitting there, with one arm resting on his knee and his chin in his palm gazing at me. The pin-striped jacket...he was wearing it. That was what I remembered most about it ,because all I could think about was a mafia movie.

"Where he was positioned in my room, it was on the furthest side, away from my door. Instantly, hoping my legs and feet were willing, I bolted out of my room to my parent's room. I woke them up by screaming. Half asleep, my mother said I had a nightmare. My stepfather, a cop, bolted for my room thinking some sick S.O.B. had broken in and was trying to molest me. As I sat with my mother, my stepfather came back after checking the room and then the doors and windows to the house and found no one had gotten in, nor was there anyone in the house. It all must have been a bad dream I thought and went back to bed. I actually fell asleep not too long after and awoke to a sunny day. Everything went as normal for the next few days, and then again one night I saw him!

"This time I was sitting at my desk doing a project for school on my typewriter, remember those things? I could see movement out of the corner of my eye, and there he was sitting on my bed. I remember looking at my new *Knight Rider* poster from the TV series which was over my bed and then shifting my gaze back to see if he was really there. He was! All he did was smirk at me in the same pinstriped suit he wore. I bolted from my bedroom screaming. By this point, my little sister who was asleep in the room next to mine was screaming too, only because I had frightened her. My stepfather checked the room and then the house, and once again there was nothing! My mother had just come home from a ladies' function, and the two sat me down and asked if I was using drugs. Something just did not add up. Yeah, no guff! I felted embarrassed and humiliated. I went to bed that night and will never forget. In the middle of the night I was awoken to something trying to pull the covers off me from the foot of my bed. I knew it was that guy in my room, no doubt. I held onto the covers tightly and didn't move. I pretended to be asleep as the covers were over my head. The tugging stopped.

"For the next two nights I felt the same tugs in the middle of the night. Finally, I started sleeping on the couch in the living room after everyone was asleep. Nothing happened while I slept on the couch, no sign of him and no tugging on my blanket. After a week, my mother made me sleep in my bed as she said the couch was bad for my back and that I was not going to turn the living room into a second bedroom. I was back in my bedroom, and I remember not being able to sleep all night!

"I had the covers pulled over my head, but remember hearing what I thought were footsteps in my bedroom as the floorboards creaked. I also felt a hand first on my feet, then a rubbing on my legs, and eventually a palm on what would have been my forehead. That last hand gesture felt like it was in place for an eternity. I remember whimpering to myself, and I think I prayed. It must have been about an hour later, not feeling anything touching me or moving around in my room, that I pulled the covers off my head as the sunlight was creeping into my bedroom. Expecting to see *HIM,* I saw an empty room. This was a Thursday night. I remember because Friday I was to leave on a school trip to Ottawa for one week. When I came back, which I worried about returning and sleeping in my bedroom, there was never any sign of him again ever, but 'ever' was not long enough because here I was now sitting across from him in 2010!

"How was this possible? What the heck was this guy? It was as if he read my mind. He picked up the DVD case and handed it to me. As I looked at it, he chuckled. *'What are you?'* I asked him. He just shrugged his shoulders. He told me that I appeared to be very frightened, that he liked me a lot, but would not hurt me, ever. He told me he was sure that I remembered him now...from my bedroom. I had indeed. It was him no doubt! He had not changed, and I am certain he had not aged a year! He handed me my designer leather coat I had brought with me and told me to put it on. He said he was taking me home.

"The car ride, which was nearly a half hour to my place, felt like an eternity. He would occasionally glance at me and smile. I said nothing. He was playing some kind of classical music on his CD player. He drove a new black Mercedes Benz. I remember the smell of the leather seats and his cologne very vividly as I sat motionless and silent. There were a few moments where I fumbled for something to say, but nothing came out. Twice he asked me if I was comfortable and if I wanted the heat on, but I only shook my head.

"When we got to my house (my sister's place), he pulled into the driveway, got out, and opened my door. I remember glancing at the clock on the dashboard. It read 3:02. Had I really been out with him that long? I know people refer to time spent as just flying by...but this was more like lost time for me. It felt more surreal, more like a dream state. He held the door open for me as I got out. He didn't try to touch me, hug me, or even kiss me goodnight. Then there was that awkward moment I will never forget and the reason I am sharing this story with you...

"I asked him what or who he was. He chuckled and stared at me for a moment, and then I saw it in his eyes. You know the coloured part of your eyes, the iris I think. Well whenever I saw his eyes, that part was brown. As he stared at me, they were almost red -- no kidding [changed actual word she used to keep this G-rated]. It was like he was possessed! With that, I bee-lined it to the door, got inside, and locked it behind me, quickly shutting off the porch light. I was going to peek out the window to see if he left, but felt nauseous and went to the bedroom I was staying in. I will be honest and tell you I didn't sleep a wink, even though I had drank a fair bit of wine. And no, I was not inebriated. I was fully aware of the night, and the conversation that transpired. I played it over and over in my mind, baffled, confused...scared! I almost expected him to show up in my room unexpected at some point throughout the night, and even looked for him, praying he would not come. He did not!

"I was off the next day. It was Sunday. I told my sister everything. She remembered the times when she was kid that I screamed there was a man in my bedroom. She reminded me how I had scared the hell out of her. She said I was doing that to her again. I never heard from him all weekend, and when I went into work Monday morning I was expecting to see him at some point, but he never came into the store. I was not disappointed! He eventually did come into the store to pick up an order about a week later, and I saw him. I was tending to another customer. He saw me and smiled at me. I thought he was going to come and talk to me, but instead I think he read from the expression on my face I wanted nothing to do with him ever again. He left!

"I have Wednesdays off. I was told he came in the following Wednesday, asked about me, and then left. He never came into the store again...I never saw him again! My sister is into some funky stuff like psychic parties and other crazy stuff. She hosted one at the house about a month after my date with this guy. We told the psychic our story, and she was very fascinated by him and what I told about him. She asked if I would mind if she did a reading for me, as well as this guy relative to me. She read the cards at least a few different times--they kept coming up the same! First, she assured my sister and me that I was telling the truth with what happened. Next, she said this European guy did not exist, at least in the human sense! When she said that, I felt my body tingle in fear. I was instantly nauseated! I will never forget the look on my sister's face. She had met him when he came to pick me up, and she said there was something not right about him. The psychic asked if I remembered where he lived. I remembered he lived in a nearby city in an older part of town in a pretty affluent neighbourhood. We planned a trip the next day, a Sunday, my sister, my brother-in-law, the psychic, and myself. I think my brother-in-law was only there to humour us and laugh at us.

"It took a while, but I found the house. There was a feature on the house which made it very easy to remember which had caught my gaze when I first saw it, and I remember staring at it from the car when we left as he took me home that night. There was no mistaking the FOR RENT sign which now rested on the front lawn. I waited in the car with my brother-in-law and my sister, and the psychic went snooping to look inside the house. Nada! The house was completely empty, all of his furnishings gone. The psychic convinced me to call the landlord to see if I could contact him because I remembered leaving something in the house. I told her I would not, but allowed my sister to do the deed. After leaving at least a few messages, the landlord returned my sister's call. My sister was told there was no way to get a hold of him, that he had moved out of the country and left no forwarding address or contact information. We also Googled his given first and last name among many other ways to find more about him, and once again NOTHING! It is as if he just doesn't exist nor ever has."

Are there such things as phantoms, ghosts that walk amongst us, or even demons? That is a good question. After speaking to these people, they seem to think so. The funny part is, I have heard a couple other similar stories along the same lines, and one was also within the Niagara Region!

KEY POINTS FROM THIS CASE

* Some people have reported experiencing the existence of phantoms-- non-corporeal beings taking on human form and communicating with them.

* Some people have tried to find birth records and reports on these so-called phantoms, and they can find no records of them.

* From the reports of people who have had these encounters, they claim that the phantom-like people they have met have remained unchanged physically even after several decades.

CHAPTER SIX

A HAUNTED THEATRE

CASES OF THE MYSTERIOUS AND MACABRE

The city of Port Colborne in Ontario, Canada boasts many wonderful attractions and scenery from its yearly Tall Ships Festival, Canal Days, beautiful marinas and fishing, to its historical theatre known as Roselawn, also called the Showboat Theatre. Built in 1860, the historical, majestic, brick and stone building still is the home to live theatre plays, as well as playing home to other fun, community activities. It is also the home to ghosts!

Niagara's Most Haunted conducted a two day shoot in the building, both getting information for an upcoming episode as well as filming re-enactments. Filming in the three-storey building, which in some way felt like being in the hotel used for Stephen King's *The Shining*, just on a smaller scale, it was easy to marvel at the breath-taking architecture, the wonderful nooks and crannies of the building, and the history of the building--a place which hosted Prime Ministers, Premiers, and Governors-General.

When you pull up to the front entry, it is hard not to notice the door with six lights of etched glass. It creates very welcoming and warming feelings walking through it. In the south hall of the building is the rose leaded glass window which reflects the craftsmanship of the entire building. I learned that the woodwork, which is amazing, is all original in the building. When you walk on the second and third floors (attic), you hear every creek and squeaking sound which adds to the ambiance of this historical building. Now comes the fun part...are the creaking sounds being caused by your own footsteps, or is it because you are being followed by something unknown to you and unseen by you? After all, this building was built in 1860. If there was an place that should be haunted, then this is the type of place, right?

I did a little research about the theatre before ever setting foot inside it as a non-patron. You see, I had been inside the Showboat Theatre over a decade ago to see a live production of a really cool play. I had no idea the theatre was supposedly haunted back then, and I didn't realize how big the Roselawn Complex really was and how many different rooms were in the building.

Roselawn Complex: Home to Showboat Theatre 2013.

Our first trip there was to interview with a high profile member of Port Colborne for an episode of *Niagara's Most Haunted*. He gave us a tour of the second level of the building and discussed how he had a meeting in Roselawn complex one evening. "It was later one evening," he told us, "and I was alone doing some paperwork in a larger room. The larger room had a great sitting room all furnished with comfy chairs, desk, tables, etc. It literally is like a small apartment. There is a room down the hallway, with the door that is always locked. In fact, the door never gets opened for anything and has not been opened for years.

"I was sitting alone in the room doing some work, and it was getting late. When you are in an older building, you hear sounds but you attribute them to the age of the building. As far as I knew, I was the only one in the building. No one had come upstairs, that I know of, as I would have definitely heard the sound of footsteps coming up the old wooden stairwell," he told us. "As far as the stairs go, when you go up them, let's just say they make a mighty loud noise and it is very hard to be discreet walking up them!

"I continued to work on what I needed to get done and then I planned on getting home," he continued. "I was getting ready to leave, and as I was walking out of the room I was in, when I heard what sounds like a voice. I got up to see who it was, and I swore I saw a foot take a step into a room and the door close behind it -- the door, that has been locked forever, that no one other than one person has the key for and has no need to go into it. I shook it off, thinking I was imaging things, so I went back to work trying to get done as I wanted to get home. About a half hour later, it happened again! I heard the voice, went to look, and once again I saw the same door close. The same foot went into that room before the door closed. Now, needless to say I was very creeped out by it and went home quickly from that facility," he said chuckling.

"The most interesting part of the story was when, about two weeks later, the manager of the Roselawn Complex approached me and asked me if we had needed use of 'the one room' that she found unlocked after being locked for the last six months. I said to her, 'No, why?' She said, 'The day after your meeting, the door had been left opened and we hadn't opened that door for the last six months.' Needless to say, the next meeting we had, there was no way I was going to be alone in there after everyone left. It was just a very creepy experience, one that I have never forgotten!"

Was this a common occurrence at the Roselawn Complex? The lady who now managed the building and theatre introduced me to a lady who had been involved with the building for practically forever! I sat down with her for an interview, and she mentioned that the place was indeed haunted.

"You definitely hear footsteps when you are alone in the building, and you know it has nothing to do with the building settling. Sometimes things get moved, and doors are opened that should not be opened. Am I frightened by these occurrences you ask? No, not at all. I think whatever is here is not harmful or trying to really scare anyone away. I think they just want to make their presence known. Have I ever seen a ghost, you ask? Yes, I have, and I have seen her on many occasion!"

This lady took me on a little tour of some of the areas of the building where she said things "happened." We came to what looked like an old bar which was now a meet and greet desk, and from there she pointed to the old, wooden, spiral staircase. "You see those stairs. That is where I usually see her looking at me."

I asked her to elaborate on what she thought was going on or what she was seeing. She continued, "I would say the ghost or apparition that I see is definitely from an older time period. She is wearing a long dress from that period. She usually stands on the small second landing where the arm rail bends into the angle and will stand and watch. She doesn't speak, and she doesn't really move. She more or less just stares or watches. No, I have never approached her or spoken to her as she is not there long enough. Within a short period of time, she just sort of dematerializes and vanishes. I would have to say I am never frightened or spooked out by these encounters. She means no harm to anyone."

There wasn't really much more I heard or much more members of my team were able to find out about the haunts in Roselawn. The building is definitely worth visiting, most definitely for live productions. It is worth seeing, if only from the outside, as it is a break-taking, historical building that has many stories to tell!

CASES OF THE MYSTERIOUS AND MACABRE

Stairwell where the lady ghost is sometimes seen.

KEY POINTS FROM THIS CASE

* Visitors and workers at the Roselawn Complex in Port Colborne report seeing the apparition of a lady in a flowing gown appearing on the staircase.

* People have reported strange occurrences such as doors opening and closing on their own when they are locked.

* The ghosts/apparitions that supposedly haunt Roselawn are not harmful and perhaps there to communicate in a playful manner.

CHAPTER SEVEN

AN OLD AND HAUNTED OPERA HALL

Lewiston, New York is one of the most picturesque towns in the entire world. Being Canadian and living near a place called Niagara on the Lake, I might be a little more biased toward my own Canadian town, but in the same breath, they are bookends to the Niagara Gorge so we can learn to appreciate both beautiful towns. Niagara on the Lake is considered one of the most haunted places in not only Canada, but in all of North America! In my book *Niagara's Most Haunted Legends and Myths*, as well as the TV series *Niagara's Most Haunted*, I have explored some of the most historical, coolest, and haunted places around. After all, the area was once host to one of the bloodiest battles in North American history between the British and the Americans in the War of 1812.

Since there were a lot of lives lost in the War of 1812, some believe that is why the area in Niagara on the Lake is so haunted. In fact, they rebuilt Fort George, the British fort, after the Americans won the war using a lot of original material, and it is a very haunted fort. In fact, it is so haunted that it also is home to some of the scariest ghost tours come the Halloween season. With that said, Fort Niagara, the American fort, is in Lewiston, and it too has been known to be haunted and host various different kinds of tours as well. While I was over in Lewiston visiting and dining at one of the fabulous little restaurants on Main Street, I learned about a really cool building on Main Street--The Lewiston Opera House or more commonly known today as Lewiston Opera Hall. And guess what? It's haunted!

The Lewiston Opera Hall was built in 1832. It was originally referred to as the Moss Hall and was built by Joseph Hewitt. It was the centre of the town, hosting dances, dinners, concerts, and balls on a regular basis. Interestingly, it was never really an opera hall. After digging into the history of the building, its claim to fame in terms of being a musical landmark came when Swedish Nightingale Jenny Lind visited the town back in the day.

What exactly is this building today? When I visited it, I recalled seeing a lawyer's office, the Art Council, new age shops, and other stores. When I spoke with a member of the Art Council and got a tour of the building, I was made aware that over the last few years, there had been a variety of paranormal investigators who had come in to the building with their equipment to conduct readings and see what they could find in the way of ghosts. This intrigued me a lot to say the least and after having an exceptional tour of the facility, the upstairs was amazing, but the basement...well you know what a basement is supposed to be about in an old historical landmark building? SCARY! And it did not disappoint. That is where my story begins...

Ole Opera Hall 2013.

After speaking with a member of the Art Council, I went off on my own and asked some folks, folks familiar with the "Ole Opera Hall" as some called it, if they had heard about ghosts and haunted things that continually went on in it. One person told me about smells or phantom odors they had heard about, one time experiencing it themselves. "I have smelled both the good and the not so good in that building. Let's start with the good...the sweet smell of lilac or something close, something that was most likely a woman's perfume, but not the kind of perfume that you would smell or find today. At my age, I remember as a little girl smelling that scent, if you will call it, whenever my granny was around. The term 'toilet water' was very popular when I was a child and I would sort of liken it to that scent. Of course I am referring to perfume, not actual toilet water. There is no mistaking the sweet, yet pungent smell of that type of perfume.

"And then there was the not so good smell I have experienced in that building, Some people said they have smelled it too, and it usually is just a flicker of a stench that passes quickly. I have smelled it a couple of times, but I thought it was my imagination until a friend said she remembers the same smell. I recall that the basement was a slaughter house, I believe, for pigs. I have been down there myself, and it looks like it was with all the thick, stone walls as well as the meat hooks I remember seeing still hanging in one of the rooms. Actually, the site kind of made me shiver inside knowing I was walking on a floor where pigs' blood must have drained. You see, I am a not a big fan of pork!" she said with a small laugh.

"I could imagine the severed carcasses of pigs hanging there, probably eyes intact peeking at you as you walk on by. I grew up outside of the area and settled here about forty years ago, but I remember hearing that pigs used to walk around with the public, much like the cats and dogs did back in the 1800's. I guess when they were big enough and when a good feeding was due, perhaps for pig roasts or needing fresh meats, they would herd them inside and slaughter them. I am glad they didn't do the same with the cats and dogs!" she said laughing.

"If there is such things as ghostly smells, just like I think there is for the perfumes I have smelled inside of the Ole Opera Hall, then I imagine there can be ghostly smells for the bad stuff, maybe slaughtered pigs? There is a sweetly, sickening stench when you smell pork flesh, one of the reasons I was turned off eating pork as a child, and there was no mistaking that smell on a couple of different occasions when I was inside that building. Like I said though, the smell is fleeting--it catches your nostrils and leaves just as fast. Luckily, the lilac smell is the one that lingers a little longer, and it makes you feel happy!"

Basement where pigs were once slaughtered.

I came across another person who told me about his experience with the scents as well, but added to what the lady had told me. He also added he had seen shadows lurking in the building--"Shadows of people that aren't there!" he said. "I have smelled certain odours in the opera hall. I have heard that others have smelled them as well. One of the more interesting stories, one I have experienced myself, is seeing shadows in the building, mainly in the stairwell leading up to the second level where they hold meetings. There was no mistaking seeing this shadowy figure.

"I remember being in the building about a decade ago waiting for my son. He had his own business and was dropping something off, and I had come to hold the front door open while he brought his order in. The order of food was going upstairs. I remember it was late afternoon, and it was also a cloudy day out. It had been raining for most of the day. As he brought the trays upstairs, I thought he was coming back down as I saw a long shadow cast on the wall. I saw this shadow coming down the stairs only I did not hear footsteps accompanying it. I found that to be weird! Then it dawned on me, there was no way there could be this shadow cast on that wall as there was no window to cast it, I mean no sunlight, and there was no sun that day, and there was not enough light to cast a shadow that didn't have a person to be the cause of the shadow.

"It didn't make sense to me when I saw it. I remember my son coming down the stairs a few minutes later and going out to get a second load of things to bring in. As I stood inside waiting for him to hold the door for him, it had started to rain lightly again. As he was unloading the van, I looked up and there it was again...this shadowy figure. And when I say figure, I mean in the form of a person or something like a person, but there was no person there to cast the shadow. When my son returned and came in, I asked him if he could see it, or had seen it, and he looked at me like I had two heads. Apparently, he saw nothing.

"I know that there are caskets in the basement. I have seen them with my own eyes. They are used for rituals for a group that occupies the building. I found that interesting, but also learned that at one point there was an undertaker who used to work from the basement back in the 1880's and prepare bodies in one area of the cellar. The cellar itself has all of these little mazes and rooms, and I think it was a small, dark, stone room where he prepared the bodies. It is kind of macabre when you think about it, but it had to be done somewhere, right? What better place than a stone cellar?

"If the basement was once used as a mortuary of any sorts, as I know it was definitely used as a slaughter house for pigs, then you would imagine if a place could or would be haunted, then this would be a prime place. The shadows on the walls were not pigs or in the shapes of pigs, just to clarify!" he said with a smile. "My wife would think I am crazy as a bird if she thought I was seeing the shadows of ghostly pigs roaming through Lewiston. No, what I saw looked like long, shadowy forms."

I dug deeper and asked around for more information. I had already heard about smells and shadows haunting the building, but did anyone actually see a ghost or anything remotely resembling something they could attribute to a human form? That was when I learned that some folks had actually reported seeing the ghost of a woman who roams the building, usually on the main level of the hall, and sometimes has been seen on the staircase leading upstairs.

From what I was able to research on this "lady ghost" that has been witnessed or seen by patrons visiting the building is dressed in period clothing from the 1800's. I had one person tell me she thought the woman looked like she was dressed in a dress that would have been popular from the Roaring Twenties. Either way, the woman ghost, who has been referred to as an apparition, was from a time period of one hundred years ago, likely longer. One of the descriptors used to refer to the lady ghost was that she was an apparition. Those who knew about this ghost stated that you are able to see her physical features pretty accurately (appearance and dress), but she is also transparent. You can see through her. Her appearances in the building are notably not as common today as they were years ago; however, she still does show up if you are one of the fortunate ones lucky enough to see her!

CASES OF THE MYSTERIOUS AND MACABRE

If you have never been to Lewiston, New York, then you are missing out on an amazing part of American history! There is so much to see in terms of aesthetic beauty, but the real treasures are found by stepping back in time and setting foot in history. Walking in buildings like the Lewiston Opera Hall bring you back to a time of our ancestors who planted the seeds of American growth and fostered the winds of change. In fact, you may not only tap into the past by feeling it, but you may see shadows from the past and scents that linger for centuries!

KEY POINTS FROM THIS CASE

* Strange odours which are from previous time periods have been reported in the Lewiston Opera Hall.

* People have reported seeing shadowy figures or moving shadows in the historical building.

* Some people have reported seeing an apparition of a lady in a dress from the late 1800's or early 1900's time period.

CHAPTER EIGHT

WHAT THE EXPERTS SAY, YOU DECIDE!

In this book, I have presented some of the more intriguing cases within the Niagara Region that examine the paranormal and activities related to them. At the end of the day, you really can't conclude or prove something that you can't see or measure. Most people would agree that they need to see it to believe it. They need actual proof!

What if there is no tangible proof, that is getting things on tape or being able to replicate the same experience? After all, for something to be scientifically proven there has to be some degree of validity, right? Even before you get to that point of testing, you would need to have a reliable measure to make sure you are testing for what it is you are truly trying to find. With that said, you have to know what it is that you are experiencing in the first place. I want to first start out with differentiating between the various entities that the people in these cases have experienced and how they are completely different.

GHOSTS

First off, let's start with the concept of ghosts. What is a ghost? Most experts in the field of paranormal investigations or religiosity would assert that a ghost is the spirit or soul of someone no longer living that can manifest itself to the living. The spirit or soul must come from a person, or animal for that matter, that once lived on this earth. The key point here is that the ghost must have first been a corporeal being that was born into the world that we live in. The next part of the ghost phenomenon is that the spirit or soul tries to consciously make contact with the living, usually loved ones or those people now living where this ghost used to live.

The common held belief amongst experts in this field is that the ghost is trying to make contact with the living because it is in a state of unrest. Some hold that the spirit or soul may be wandering earth because it has not crossed over to the "other side" or does not know how to get there. Others believe that the spirit or soul may not even think that it is dead!

Throughout history, there have been both religious and psychical beliefs discerning "the white light" or white light experience needed to cross over to the other side, this being Heaven or the afterlife. Experts who believe in ghosts haunting places on Earth assert that spirits or souls are trapped in this world (corporeal world) and need to get to the non-corporeal world (the other side). Some psychics and mediums believe that these spirits need to be guided or coaxed to go to the light so they can get to the other side, where they are supposed to be. The reasoning as to why they have not crossed over varies according to some psychics and mediums. Some believe that they just do not want to leave this world because they are fearful to cross over. One theory is that the spirit believes it has unfinished business in this world and does not want to move on. It may believe it has to stay to watch over the loved ones and then eventually gets trapped and does not know how to move on. Then there are those who believe that the spirit, while living, suffered a tragic or sudden death and for some reason just has not accepted it is dead or is not able to move on.

When you bring up the concept or notion of ghosts with experts in this field, they will tell you the following. First, some ghosts can be very playful or very malicious! They have the ability to have an influence on the lives of the living and can torment them. Second, most stay or remain in the places where they spent most of their time in their daily lives while they were living. Some ghosts do not like intruders -- the living -- moving into their place! Most times, ghosts will try to get one's attention to either tell them something, give them a message, or scare them away. They really can't do much harm other than spook someone. It is believed that ghosts cannot lift heavy objects or throw things at the living.

Finally, ghosts have to be asked, coaxed, or coerced to leave and go to the light. Some researchers state that when you take authority over the place you own in this world and tell the ghost they have to leave or move on, then they do leave. Furthermore, those who are religious may ask a clergy person to help guide the ghost away by praying for them or over them and releasing them from this world.

APPARITIONS

Apparitions often times get confused with ghosts as being one in the same. An apparition is the appearance of something that once lived (human, plant, or animal) with no material stimulus or matter for it to actually be able to exist. In essence, the apparition appears to be nothing more than a mist or a vapour-like substance. Experts in this area of study assert that the apparition may very much appear to look like or be a ghost, but it is not the same.

First off, apparitions cannot influence their environment by moving things. They are just there to literally play out a movement or an action sequence, and this sequence of actions is usually repetitious -- the same thing done over and over again. The reason that the apparition replays the same scene over and over again is because that is usually the last thing they were doing before dying, or what they did often, or had intense feelings attached to while they were living. Much like ghosts, apparitions were once on Earth in human form, but the only difference is they are not a spirit or soul, rather a remnant of former human energy.

Second, apparitions are not aware of the living. You could scream at an apparition or try to touch it, and it will not acknowledge you or try to influence you because it is unaware of you. Furthermore, apparitions cannot lift or move things. They do not have the conscious energy to do so. In fact, some experts believe that apparitions only exist for those who are sensitive in that they can see things other people cannot see. The belief is that whatever has lived possessed energy, which is an absolute fact. This energy imprints itself on the universe, thus creating a "Polaroid photo" effect, meaning it is in the history of the world. These Polaroid effects could be in the form of moving pictures, like a film. Sensitive people like psychics are able to tap into the universal ether and see these moving pictures or apparitions.

Moreover, some experts in the field assert that people who see apparitions are projecting their own perceptions outwardly to create these apparitions. The apparitions only exist for them and only they can see them because it is their mind that created them. In essence, there is no such thing as the apparition for anyone else, only the one seeing it because they created it!

On the other hand, when there are several people who see the same apparition (a non spiritual entity or ghost) then they may in fact be seeing this residual imprint in universal ether playing itself out before their eyes like a silent movie. Since the apparition cannot make noise, cannot move things, cannot communicate, and is unaware of the living, it would basically look like a silent movie. Once more, some paranormal experts would contend that the reason this is happening is that the living person was snatched from life so fast and moved onto the other side, but this residual energy from when they were alive is replaying itself.

POLTERGEISTS

A poltergeist is not a ghost or an apparition. Poltergeist is a German term, and when you translate it, it means "noisy ghost". This translation often times confuses people into thinking that poltergeists are ghosts. With poltergeists, the common occurrences include activities such as banging, knocking, flickering lights, objects being knocked over, things falling off walls, doors being opened, feeling touched, and even what sound like apparent human voices.

Poltergeist activity is not from ghosts or apparitions, rather from living people. According to paranormal researchers, poltergeist activity is based on psychokinesis, which is the ability to move things with the human mind. The interesting part of this is that most individuals possessing psychokinetic abilities and are able to manifest poltergeists do so unknowingly!

Some theorists believe that poltergeist activity usually involves kids or teens, prior to reaching puberty. These kids are angry, depressed, or could be victims of abuse, and they project their "rage" outwards and make these noisy spirits happen. Damage or attacks (things falling over on people in the same vicinity of the subject) often times occur unconsciously by the subject. Yes, they are angry, and they displace their rage but really can't control the targets they are aiming for or don't even know that they are aiming!

There are schools that study and train people to harness their psychokinetic and psychic abilities. The extent to how effective and strong these abilities are is very debatable! Furthermore, some experts who study paranormal activity and poltergeists assert that these occurrences are nothing more than the influences of electromagnetic fields. Then there are those subscribing to religion and assert that it is demonic influence.

DEMONIC INFLUENCE

When discussing demons or demonic influence, you are getting into the realm of religion. Perhaps one first has to believe in a Heaven and Hell and in God and the devil for demons to be accepted as a legitimate explanation.

What do we know about demons based on religious teachings? First, demons were created along with the angels. In fact, they were with the angels as angels themselves! When Lucifer, the most majestic angel created along with Michael and Gabriel, challenged God for supremacy, he was cast out of heaven along with 1/3 of his angel followers. He was named Satan, the father of lies, and his 1/3 supporting staff became his demons and minions. These demons were never in human form, and many feeling the shame and pain of exile and disconnection from the Divine, wish to not only possess humans, so they can get into a warm body, but also destroy the beauty that God has created.

In most religions, the belief is that a demon cannot possess a person or maintain residency in a house/apartment unless it is willingly invited. The most obvious way to invite a demon in is to ask it through worship or prayer. If someone is a member of an occult group that practices demonic worship, they probably have a first class ticket to getting what they want--a possession! Then there is the belief that demons can show up and stay through occult practicing/black magic, even in unsuspecting people doing it. You see, they conjure up a demon or control it without even knowing they are doing so. Some people even conjure them up while just having fun or playing around with Ouija boards, Tarot cards, séances, or fortune tellers who claim to be communicating with angels or deceased loved ones. The demon pretends to be a nice spirit, a wolf in sheep's clothing, and tricks people into getting into their lives. Do you actually think something disgusting and hideous would appear in that form and expect to be welcomed in?

Once the demon comes into someone's world/life, they can make life for them a living hell, pun intended! It is believed that demons dislike the light as well as religious articles such as the Crucifix, rosaries, and other blessed objects. Most of their assaults begin after midnight and last through the night. Much like poltergeists, there is a lot of noises and banging, knocking (usually in 3's to mock the Holy Trinity-Father, Son and Holy Ghost), objects being moved or destroyed, lights flashing, birds flying into houses, rocks falling out of the skies onto homes, disgusting odours that linger, intense temperature changes, dark figures appearing, loud voices and screams, and even physical assaults.

It is believed that demons get into a person's life through an infestation--the demon haunts the person in their dwelling. They make it known they are there and try to get the individual to attend to them or give them some sort of attention. The next goal of the demonic entity is oppression--here the demon tries to launch a series of psychological or physical attacks to wear the individual down and cause them to become physically, mentally, emotionally, and spiritually weak. As this diabolical siege continues, the goal of the demon is to continue the oppression until the individual becomes extremely weak. They resign their free will and become open to demonic possession!

When possessions occur, it is at that point that experts in exorcisms or the church need to be called in to help the individual(s) being assaulted or possessed. There are extremely mixed beliefs on whether or not it is a real possession or a mental illness that the individual possesses. I am not here to state it one way or the other, just to go over the beliefs on these occurrences. Also, I am not an expert in these matters, nor do I want the first hand experience that would come with learning about them. Being amongst the living is enough for me, and "spiritually" possessed with a fine wine, dark ale, or exceptional mixed drink is about my speed!

With that said, I have read the work based on Ed and Lorraine Warren's work with demonic possessions and ghosts. Ed and Lorraine are famous for working on cases such as the Amityville Horror in the 1970's as well as other famous cases. Recently a movie called *The Conjuring* (2013) was based on one of their most intense cases of possession and contains frightening actual accounts from beginning to end! If you have never heard of the Warrens, I strongly recommend Googling them. Their cases have been authenticated, and they have hard physical evidence!

One last note on Ed Warren which is interesting! I remember reading somewhere some time ago, that Ed stated (after working on many cases involving haunts, poltergeists, and demons) that ghosts and poltergeists cannot lift or move heavy objects. Interestingly, if I recall, I think he mentioned 2 pounds or more (don't shoot me for getting this wrong, research it for yourself) cannot be moved by ghosts or poltergeists.

There, I have presented the cases and also given you information on what the majority of experts believe (that is the experts who believe in the paranormal and spiritual world). At the end of the day, which makes it the dark of night, it is up to you to decide what you truly want to believe!

*To Learn more about Niagara's Most Haunted TV Series as well as some of the most haunted places in North America, visit: www.niagarasmosthaunted.com or read about where it all got started in Niagara's Most Haunted: Legends and Myths today!

"Niagara's Most Haunted brings to light the 'unmentionables' and the hauntings that are known of in Niagara."
— Jim Diodati, Mayor of Niagara Falls

NIAGARA'S MOST HAUNTED

Legends and Myths

Peter Andrew Sacco

FORWARD BY GORDON DEPPE
LEAD SINGER OF CANADA'S CELEBRATED BAND THE SPOONS

"Niagara's Most Haunted provides insight and intrigue to Ontarians and visitors alike to explore and experience the darker side of what Niagara has to offer as a truly dynamic destination."
— Kim Craitor, MPP Niagara Falls

Do you like horror stories? Read on and get a taste of Peter's scary short story "THE CLOSET" from his popular selling book FEAR FACTORS, guaranteed to keep you awake at nights!

Excerpt from Fear Factors:
THE CLOSET

Jean Thomas winced in pain as the wooden screen door grazed her fingertips when it blew shut. She dropped the box of pots and pans she was holding and they clanged loudly against the wooden banister at the base of the stairs. There was a moment of silence before two teenage children came running down the stairs. Billy Thomas, Jean's twelve year old son was the first to reach the bottom. Clair, his seventeen-year old sister, was not far behind.

"Are you okay, mom?" asked a concerned Clair.

Jean managed to shake the numbness from her fingertips.

"What happened?" asked a smiling Billy.

"The damn door blew shut and got my hand."

"Oh, mom. You really should be more careful. Isn't that what you are always telling us?" quipped Clair.

"What's going on upstairs?" asked Jean.

"Well, we've got most of the stuff put in the proper rooms. We're going to need some help moving the wardrobe," responded Clair with a sigh.

Jean picked the box of pots and pans off the floor and carried them into the kitchen. The hallway leading to the kitchen was quite narrow. Strips of old wallpaper, dangling from walls, brushed Jean's hair as she went into the kitchen. Billy followed close behind, ripping the shreds of paper from the walls.

"Don't do that!" objected Clair slapping Billy's arm.

"Why? It's all coming down anyway," snapped Billy.

"Mom, will you tell him to stop it?"

Jean removed one of the pans from the box and placed it on the stove. "Will you kids cool it. I thought we promised no arguing for a while." Jean took a couple of eggs from the tray in the refrigerator and scrambled them in a bowl. "Are the two of you hungry yet?"

"Eggs again?" winced Billy.

"Just shut up and eat what you're given," rejoined Clair.

Jean offered Billy a dissatisfied look and he smiled. "Eggs will be just fine, mom."

Jean began to prepare the meal, as Clair prepared a tomato salad. Billy sat down at the table, which was surrounded by a fortress of boxes. He took a comic book from one of the boxes and began to read it. Pleasantly, Jean hummed to herself as she fried the omelet. Clair peered out the kitchen window as she prepared her salad and noticed a boy about Billy's age playing at the end of their driveway. The boy was almost knee deep in the neglected, meadow-deep grass. Clair glanced at her mother. She still appeared very young for a thirty-seven-year old mother of two. She had kept herself very fit and trim and her curly blonde hair hid any hints of gray that may have tried to break through. The sadness which dominated her baby blues for so long following the long, drawn-out divorce from Clair's father, now seemed far removed. Perhaps it was the move from Boston to Santa Barbara that had been the true healer. Even though it was less than a week, their lives felt fresh and new. Clair still missed her father. Even though Billy did not say anything, she knew he too missed his dad and their friends back home.

Jean Thomas had the chance for a job transfer to either Santa Barbara, or Georgia; and she chose Santa Barbara in an instant. The decision was an easy one, although the kids were against it throughout the entire process; but she figured they would adjust once they were moved. Besides, what kid, or adult for that matter, did not dream about living in California at least once?

Jean's job with the computer programming company in Boston was by no means in jeopardy even though the divorce had waged on for nearly two years and had started to drain her. It was very visible to her boss, Mr. Harnish and co-workers. It was Mr. Harnish who had suggested she take some time off from work and get away for a while. Jokingly, she had asked if he could transfer her to the other side of the planet, with seniority and full benefits intact. He said the best he could do was Santa Barbara. At first she thought he was kidding. Later she found out he was quite serious. He said he wished she wouldn't consider the transfer, as with over fourteen years service, she was one of his best programmers. He said he would understand if she left, given the trying pressures which were overwhelming her mentally, emotionally and physically.

Her soon-to-be ex-husband, Bob, had been trying to get custody of the kids. She knew, and her lawyer knew, he didn't have a snowball's chance in hell. Bob, however, the asshole he truly was, thought he would make things difficult by not co-operating in doing what was best for the children. Jean thought he was the lowest form of scum on the earth.

Bob was a salesman, and to this very day, she still did not know what the hell he sold. He was very good at selling himself though. At forty-two, Bob thought he was still God's gift to women and why not let the babes enjoy his youth while he still had it? Bob was balling several of his female clients in between appointments. Jean lost count after she caught him the fourth time. She thought the third time was always the charm. How he ever conned her again into giving him another chance was still a mystery. He used the children to manipulate her. She had enough of his shit. Her job at work was enough stress, let alone having to deal with the ego of her adolescent husband. She told him and the kids she had had enough. She told Bob she was filing for a divorce and getting on with her life. The kids cried as expected, but not for long, as they had somehow expected it was for real this time. Bob had pleaded once more in his groveling, childish manner, but it didn't work. When he realized it was for real, he said the kids were going to stay with him. Not! Eventually, the courts, including his own lawyer saw what an ass he was and the case was closed. A real estate agent for the company Jean worked for found her an older, smaller house, in the suburbs of Santa Barbara. It was then "California or bust?" for the Thomas clan.

The house was a century old and two-levels. Even though it appeared very rough around the edges, it had amazing potential. The house reminded Jean of the house she had lived in as a little girl. The exterior of the house was surprisingly well kept. The red bricks preserved their deep richness throughout the years. The yard outside was on the verge of becoming a weed field with a variety of litter blowing through thick, matted growth. Jean figured if she were especially nice to the kids, they might have it cleaned up in a week or so. The inside of the house was another matter. Most of the walls either had to be re-plastered or repainted. To Jean's surprise, some of the paint and wallpaper in the house was original.

The original wood floors were somewhat dull from years of living, although nothing a bottle of wax could not fix. The ceiling in one of the bedrooms leaked during periods of heavy rain. Some of the black shingles on the roof had begun to curl and needed replacing. Wooden supports in the attic had started to rot from the persistent rains throughout the years. And of course, the house had its fair share of rodents. Nothing an exterminator could not fix. Other than that, the house was a real gem. Jean honestly thought the house was great and their lives here would flourish.

An older lady, Sarah Miller, now deceased, had owned the house as far back as anyone could remember. One of the stories Jean had heard was Miller had been a very respected artist and after she had moved into the house her career came to an abrupt end. She was quite renowned for her flower and fruit bowl paintings. When the house became the state's property following her death, they found paintings which were very disturbing and bordered on the grotesque.

In many of the paintings, a man holding an ax was depicted. It was the same man in all of her paintings. Most of the paintings showed the man cutting the heads off chickens. In one very disturbing painting, the man appeared to have chopped the head off a woman tied to a tree stump. Several art critics found Miller's work very bizarre and out of character. They could not believe she would paint such pictures. It was later revealed the man in the paintings greatly resembled her father. He had been a chicken farmer in the early nineteen hundreds, but was killed in the line of duty during the first World War.

The Miller family had owned a farm in the Midwest and moved to California following the war to get their lives back in order. The husband's brother had owned the house and had offered to take the family in. Even more shocking was the fact Sarah Miller moved back into the house following her mother's murder. From what the coroner's report stated, the mother was beheaded. There was much speculation about the murder but the killer was never caught. There were no fingerprints nor any leads to go on. Sarah chose to live in her mother's house like a hermit.

She never really mingled with the neighbors. Some of them claimed that mentally, Sarah was a tree short of a trunk. On one occasion, Sarah had talked about how she would prepare meals for her father and take them to him. She also claimed her deceased father had killed her mother for not remaining faithful to him. No one really knew the story for sure, nor for that matter, what had really happened. As far as Jean was concerned, this was home for her and her children now. No old wives' tale was going to scare them away from living in this house. Besides, she had her own horror story living back east. Hopefully, he would stay there.

The Thomas clan pretty well had all their belongings moved into the house. Most of the furniture had been placed in their desired locations. Billy was the happiest of the two children. He had gotten the room his sister had wanted. It was the largest room in the house. It was a bedroom attached to a step-up attic. The attic was converted into a loft for the bedroom. His bed rested in the tiny loft and the dresser and computer were situated in the bedroom. Billy called his bedroom "a real pad." Clair had made several waves about wanting the room, but surrendered her hostilities when she noticed the two of them were wearing down their mother's already thin patience. Case closed. Billy got the room. Clair's room was much smaller, but she had the sun to wake her every morning through the small bay window. Being an avid lover of the sun, this compensated her somewhat. Jean was very happy with the everyday, run of the mill, master bedroom.

THE CLOSET

The family had been living in the unfurnished house for just about a week. The last two nights in the house had been less than restful for Billy. Around two in the morning, he had been awakened from his sleep by sounds like loud dripping. Whenever he turned his light on, however, the dripping disappeared. He thought it might be Clair trying to frighten him out of the bedroom. That theory was quickly dispelled when he spied on her in her bedroom and watched her sleeping soundly. Billy investigated the room for leaks but was unable to find any. The faucets in the bathroom down the hall were turned off. It was not raining outside. Where the hell was the noise coming from?

Billy thought maybe, an old pipe of some sort was leaking in the roof, but where would the water be coming from at that time of night? No one was using water this late. Actually, the sound first appeared to becoming from the closet in the corner of his loft. When Billy opened the closet door, he expected water to be all over the small floor. There wasn't even a drop. The floor was dry and the walls were dry. There was not even a drop of perspiration on the brick wall at the end of the closet.

Billy unscrewed the light bulb at the top of the closet and shut the door perplexed. As soon as he went back to bed the dripping sound started again. Damn closet, he thought. Billy did not like closets anyway and this one gave him the creeps whenever it was opened. Perhaps it was the old red brick wall staring at him which made him uneasy. It reminded him of a movie he watched with his father when he was younger. In that movie, St. Valentine's Day Massacre, there had been a large brick wall. The blood on the wall had really scared the shit out of him. Now whenever the closet door was opened and the red brick wall was staring at him, he could swear he saw blood crying from the cracks in the bricks. He vowed to himself he would never again watch that movie for as long as he lived. The closet was useless and why did it have to be in his pad? There were no shelves or hooks to store anything, so why have it? Jean told Billy she was going to store her china and silverware in there. She could have all she wanted of that closet, thought Billy. He had his own closet in the room below.

The next morning, Billy told his mother of the dripping noise coming from the closet the last two nights. Jean and Clair both claimed they had heard nothing. Jean checked all of the faucets and ceilings for leaks but found nothing. Clair teased Billy about the noise and told him she would be more than happy to change bedrooms with him. That was all he had to hear. He would discuss the dripping noise no more. Clair placed the plates down on the table and Jean tossed omelets into each of them. Jean swiped the comic book from Billy's hands and tossed it onto the counter. Before they began to eat, Jean said grace. Billy dove into his omelet.

"For someone who was sick of eggs, you're sure doing all right there," smiled Jean.

Clair got a soda from the refrigerator. "Do we really have to start school next month?" she asked less than enthusiastic.

"You are children and children do attend school," Jean smiled.

"I wonder what the schools are going to be like out here?" asked Billy.

"I'm sure they are no different from what they were like in Boston," answered Jean.

"I was afraid of that," quipped Clair.

"Oh, I'm sure you'll both make a lot of friends at school in Santa Barbara."

"That's real comforting," snorted Clair, through a full mouth of food.

"Don't worry, Sis, I'm sure you'll have a boyfriend soon," smirked Billy.

"Why don't you keep your mouth shut when you are eating?" asked Clair raising her voice impatiently.

Billy opened his mouth to expose the food. Clair winced at him and offered him a provocative finger.

"Now cut it out, both of you and act your ages. I'm sure you will make plenty of friends out here, and you'll both survive. If I'm going to, so will you," sighed Jean.

Billy glanced at Clair and she shrugged. Silently, they finished eating.

***

Jerry Webb, the dark-haired boy who had been playing in the tall grass at the end of Thomas' driveway, now sat on the curb lacing up his in-line skates. Billy came out of the house and stood on the porch watching him. Jerry struggled to keep his balance as he climbed to his feet. As he tried to skate away from the curb, he stumbled comically from one foot to the other over a manhole cover. Still wavering back and forth, his legs were thrown up forward like a rag doll, and he landed on his butt in the middle of the street. Billy burst out laughing. Jerry looked back over his shoulder and saw Billy standing there laughing at him. He walked over to where Jerry was lying on the street and helped him to his feet. As Jerry climbed to his feet, he nearly fell once more, pulling Billy down with him. Billy tentatively dragged

Jerry over to the side of the road and placed him down on the grass, and breathed a sigh of relief.

"Skate much?" Billy asked sarcastically.

***DOWNLOAD FEAR FACTORS TODAY or BUY IT IN PAPERBACK!

http://www.amazon.com/FEAR-FACTORS-Peter-Andrew-Sacco/dp/1591132231/ref=sr_1_1?s=books&ie=UTF8&qid=1380904327&sr=1-1&keywords=Fear+Factors+Peter+Sacco

"One heck of a great read!... One Hell Of A Sexy Deal was erotically scary. I loved it!"
— D.J. Carl, Horrorwood Babbleon

Fear Factors

REVISED EDITION
containing the new short story *Tormented*

Peter Andrew Sacco

Fear Factors is a book about man's inhumanity to man--It's about the evil man does. Basically, it's how some humans create hell for others! How far are you willing to push the envelope to get what you really, really want at the expense of another person?

Fear Factors contains 11 short stories/novellas which are guaranteed to keep you up at night--reading, or afraid to turn the lights off. Vampires, ghosts, demons, Hitler, urban legends and infidelity are the ingredients for nightmarish tales. Fear Factors has the horrific ingredients and more to satiate the true horror lover's taste buds! Are you up for these horrific reads?

"Frightening, intense, provocative, stylish... A cunning imagination!"
— Maple Tree Productions

Peter Andrew Sacco is also the author of *The Lost Fountain, Midnight Eclipse, Jack or Jill* and *Second Time Around*. He resides in Niagara Falls, Canada. Visit Peter at **www.petersacco.com**

Cover images:
© Elisanth_Dreamstime.com (dead girl);
© Nikhil Gangavane_Dreamstime.com (wall & face)

ISBN 978-1-59113-223-3
90000

9 781591 132233